Machine Learning for Beginners

A Complete and Phased Beginner's Guide to Learning and Understanding Machine Learning and Artificial Intelligence

By: Ethem Mining

Table of Contents

Introduction

While many people have heard about "artificial intelligence" or AI, not as many people seem to know what machine learning is. With that being said, machine learning is a subfield of AI and is, in many cases, the basis for AI technology. The goal of machine learning technology is to understand the structure of data and fit that data into specific models that are able to then be understood and used by humans for various applications throughout life. Machine learning is recognized as a field of computer sciences, however it does not carry the same approach that traditional computer sciences carry. Whereas traditional computer sciences are driven with algorithms that are human-created and managed, machine learning is driven by algorithms that the device itself can learn from and grow from. Beyond that, they are often built with a very specific purpose that enables them to specialize in specific areas of "knowledge" or capabilities.

These days, anyone who has used technology has benefitted from the power of machine learning in one way or another as it has become built into common, everyday technologies. Devices such as your cell phone, tablet, smart watch, computer, and other smart devices have all been designed using the power of smart technology, or machine learning technology. Everything from the face recognition capabilities in your phone to the self-driving technology in cars is derived from specialized forms of machine learning technology. It has become, and continues to become, a highly relevant and well-researched part of our modern world.

The more we continue to develop new technologies and put these new technologies to work in our modern society, the more we are putting machine learning to work for us. As a result, computer scientists continue to research machine learning capabilities and expand on this unique form of technology so that they can be used in newer and even more revolutionary devices.

In this book, *Machine Learning for Beginners,* I want to elaborate on what machine learning is, exactly, how it works, and why it is something that people need to educate themselves more on. Whether you are a computer scientist or aspiring computer scientist yourself, or if you are a technology enthusiast, I hope that you will find great value in what you learn here within this book. Inside we are going to cover everything to help you begin to understand machine learning and it's many uses so that you can develop confidence in what it is that you are talking about, and learning about, when discussing machine learning technology.

As you read through this book, please note that the primary goal is to help you learn about and understand machine learning. This particular topic is an incredibly vast topic with a seemingly endless number of subfields and areas of focus, all of which are devoted to different methods of advancing or utilizing this particular technology. For that reason, there is no way that I could possibly discuss every single aspect of machine learning technology in a single book.

However, with this foundational knowledge you will be able to take your basic understanding of machine learning and use it to develop even more knowledge in your chosen area of research, should you desire to pursue machine learning in any way. So, if you are ready to get started, let's begin!

Chapter 1: What is Machine Learning?

In the introduction, we briefly touched into what machine learning is exactly. In its essence, machine learning is a form of computer science technology whereby the machine itself has a complex range of "knowledge" that allows it to take certain data inputs and use complex statistical analysis strategies to create output values that fall within a specific range of knowledge, data, or information.

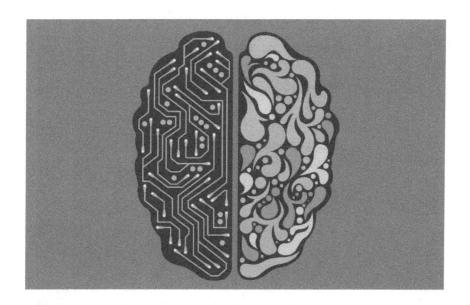

This sounds complex, and that is because it is. However, once you begin digging into what machine learning is exactly it becomes easier to understand how this particular technology works and what can be done with it. In order to help you really start to dig into machine learning, we are going to start with the very basics. That is: what machine learning is, the history of it, what it can do and how it is applied, what benefits it has, and practical everyday examples of how machine learning is used.

Definition of Machine Learning

The definition of machine learning is one that is relatively difficult to summarize because it is often described or explained differently by different people, or groups.

With that being said, the generally agreed upon definition of machine learning is: *"machine learning focuses on the development of computer programs that can access data and use it to learn for themselves."*

Machine learning devices essentially take data, and use to look for patterns and other pieces of specified information to create predictions or recommendations. The goal is for computers to learn how to use data and information to be able to learn automatically, rather than requiring humans to intervene or assist with the learning process.

In other words, rather than having to push updates or adjust the coding, machine learning devices should be able to recognize its own "needs" and "learn" the upgrades accordingly. This means that the device itself would be able to create and push its own updates and become more functional based on what it was meant to do in the first place.

With that being said, this definition is not always entirely accurate, as there are different types of machine learning methods. Some of them, such as the ones described previously, is completely unsupervised and should require absolutely no human intervention to be able to function and learn or evolve entirely on their own. Others, however, require moderate to consistent supervision to ensure that they are operating properly. We will discuss more these different categories of learning methods in Chapter 2, when you can discover what each one means and when that particular learning method would be applied to a machine learning device.

History of Machine Learning

Machine learning may seem like new technology, especially because we are now starting to see more "futuristic" devices in play with our smartphones and our cars fostering more advanced forms of technology.

With that being said, the concept of machine learning is certainly not new, and has actually been around for exactly six decades at the time of *Machine Learning for Beginners* being written and released. That means that the term "machine learning" was first introduced in 1959!

The term machine learning was introduced by Arthur Samuel when he worked at IBM back in the 1950s and 1960s. Samuel was an American pioneer when it came to computer gaming and artificial intelligence, and has largely been recognized as the original inventor of the concept of machine learning. Following his discovery and description of machine learning, Nils J. Nilsson released a book called Learning Machines that discussed the earliest forms of machine learning as we know it today. Back then, these machines were ultimately capable of recognizing patterns and classifying them. At the time, it was a massive move toward something new, but looking back just 60 years later it seems like such a basic form of the machine learning technology we have grown used to in today's world.

Throughout the 1970s and 1980s, machine learning technology was continually upgraded to identify even more patterns and categorize them more effectively. At this point, computers and the internet were not yet a common staple in the average American household, so this technology was still largely private amongst computer scientists and engineers. Later, in the 1990s, computers became more popular in the average household and machine learning was starting to make its way into people's everyday lives.

By the time computers were becoming more popular, systems had begun to be put into play so that computers could mine data. This way, anyone who was plugged into the internet could, technically, "feed the machine" so to speak by allowing their devices, and other devices, to collect data about their computer usage habits.

This lead to the devices being able to create more favorable experiences over time, such as with search engines being able to offer more relevant search results, or more recently with social media platforms being able to customize advertisements for users.

As machine learning capabilities have continued to grow over time, we have seen our lives being massively impacted by them. At this point, machine learning is used to optimize the functionality of computers and their software, has helped build statistics and growth, and has helped customize user's experiences on the internet, and with other software they might use.

The Future of Machine Learning

The scope of machine learning, or the future of machine learning, is still largely unknown. At this point, we can only prophesize what we think is going to happen, however the future is looking rather incredible with machine learning included. There are many ways that machine learning will be included in the future of our world, in ways that can touch nearly every area of our lives. Machine learning could come to affect everything from the way we shop to the way we commute, and even the way we interact with each other or with our technology. At this point, anything is possible.

Some of the futuristic ideas that computer scientists have come up with include things like ending the industrialized era so that we can allow AI to completely run our industries.

Many argue that this would be far cleaner than using fossil fuels and human labor like we have been using to date. For many machine learning could indicate freedom from lives that have otherwise been spent engaged in active labor for decades upon decades. In a time where many struggles to even retire, machine learning could enable the entire working class a new lease on life, so to speak. As people engaged in work-free lives, they could also use technology like completely self-driving cars, digital assistants, and other smart city technology. In many ways, the machine learning we are coming to know will transform finances, manufacturing, shopping, media, and even the healthcare industry.

We could see changes in how we track, manage, and use our money, and how we shop altogether. We could see our products being manufactured completely by AI.

As well, we will likely see machine learning technologies continue to customize the media we see and how it is presented to us so that we are consuming media in a more enjoyable manner. In the healthcare industry, you could see anything from better personal healthcare information monitoring systems to better technology that can be used for diagnosing and discovering illnesses or abnormalities in people's health. So much can be moved over to machine learning technology and changed as we know it, as long as we continue to explore it and learn how to practically apply it to our world. Many people think that we are in for an AI revolution. At this rate, we would find ourselves amongst a completely new era were, rather than being fueled by the foundation of the industrial revolution, we would be fueled by the AI revolution.

In this sense, modern fuels, manufacturers, factories, and even engines and transportation forms as we know them would become obsolete as the AI era took over instead.

While we cannot claim that this would be the perfect revolution, chances are it would support us in healing much of the problems that fossil fuels and carbon emissions have caused to our planet. In many ways, it may be the revolution we require in order to undo the damage that the industrial revolution has done to our planet.

Application of Machine Learning

To date, there are 44 different ways that machine learning has been applied in our modern world. These different applications have served in two different ways. On one level, they have provided computer scientists with the opportunity to discover, explore, and understand how machine learning technology can work in different applications of our modern world. In many cases, these aspects of research remain private and have yet to be introduced to or used by the public. On another level, these applications are regularly being interacted with and used by the public as a way to help revolutionize and evolve our way of living. This is both an opportunity for us to implement and enjoy new technology, while also being able to get a feel for how well this machine learning technology holds up in massive ways. The more successfully it is applied and used by the general public, the stronger the technology becomes and the more it can be applied in other areas of life, too.

So far, the 44 applications of technology involve being used in industries such as the technology industry, the agricultural industry, the medical industry, the financial industry, the marketing industry, and even the human behavior industry. Below is a breakdown of where machine learning has been applied in each of these industries.

Technology Industry

- Adaptive websites
- Affective computing
- Computer networks
- Computer vision
- Data quality
- General game playing
- Information retrieval
- Internet fraud detection
- Machine learning control
- Machine perception
- Machine translation
- Optimization
- Recommender systems
- Robot locomotion
- Search engines
- Sequence Mining
- Software engineering

- Speech recognition
- Syntatic pattern recognition
- Telecommunication
- Theorem proving
- Time series forecasing

Agricultural Industry

- Agriculture

Medical Industry

- Anatomy
- Bioinformatics
- Brain-machine interfaces
- Cheminformatics
- DNA sequence classification
- Medical diagnosis
- Structural health monitoring

Financial Industry

- Banking
- Credit-card fraud detection
- Economics

- Financial market analysis
- Insurance

Marketing Industry

- Marketing
- Online advertising

Human Behavior Industry

- Handwriting recognition
- Linguistics
- Natural language processing
- Natural language understanding
- Sentiment analysis
- User behavior analytics

Benefits of Machine Learning

You can find a vast number of benefits from machine learning no matter where you look. These benefits can be categorized by industry, or looked at as an entire series of benefits from machine learning itself.

Because this book is about machine learning in general, and is not biased to any specific industry, we are going to look at some of the many benefits of machine learning as a whole. If you want to go even deeper into understanding the benefits of machine learning, take a look at machine learning for the industry that you are most interested in to find ample benefits relating to that particular industry.

One of the biggest advantages of machine learning is that it makes identifying trends and patterns incredibly simple. Trends and patterns are important in many types of data, ranging from medical records to behaviors, and even demographics and other basic information. Having a machine capable of both tracking or mining and reading over the data makes identifying trends and patterns much easier. In the past, trends and patterns had to be looked over by humans through having humans search through massive amounts of information.

This could take days, weeks, and even months or longer depending on how much data was available, and was often inaccurate as people could easily overlook pieces of information and miss trends or patterns. Computers, however, using machine learning technology can identify patterns and trends in minutes after searching through hundreds of thousands, of not millions of pieces of data.

Another benefit of machine learning is that there is no need for human intervention, which means that the devices can continually improve themselves using automated behaviors.

Having devices that are capable of completing complex tasks on their own, without the intervention of humans, and with their own continuous improvement means that we can start seeing massive changes in the way technology is developed. To date, technology has been designed by human brains which, while incredibly imaginative and productive, are also highly prone to error. The human brain can also miss things, or struggle to identify new patterns, trends, or needs when something stops working.

This means it could take months or even years for developments to be made exclusively through the human mind. With the application of machine learning devices, this time can be minimized and the process of evolving technology can be further simplified as technology ultimately beings improving itself.

In addition to the aforementioned, machine learning can be applied to a wide variety of applications, and can handle multiple different aspects of information or developments. As mentioned earlier, machine learning can revolutionize everything from how we shop to how we diagnose and treat medical illnesses, or even implement government programs. When we have machine learning fully tapped into and in force, we can use it to improve virtually everything in our modern world in such a way that we will find ourselves experiencing life different from how we know it to be today.

Practical Examples of Everyday Use of Machine Learning

Machine learning already exists in so many areas of our modern lives. To help you get a feel for what a life with machine learning looks like, let's look at nine different ways that machine learning is already being practically applied to our modern world so that you can begin to understand how, and why, it works. Through recognizing machine learning capabilities in your own world, you will likely see just how powerful and useful this particular form of technology is.

One big way that machine learning has been introduced in the past few years is through image recognition. These days, many smart phones, tablets, gaming devices, and even computers are capable of recognizing certain faces and doing things based on what they see. For example, your smart phone may have image recognition technology that enables it to unlock anytime you look at your device.

Another way that machine learning technology has been implemented is through speech recognition. For just under a decade now we have been using speech recognition as a way to interact with our devices to request support, launch applications, and even use our smart phones while we are driving. Speech recognition is continuing to be implemented more and more with the development of in-home "smart assistants" such as Google Home, Alexa, and Apple's Home Pod.

Machine learning has also been applied to medical diagnosis already, with machines being developed that can screen patients using various tests or collections of data to help identify possible ailments that the individual may have. So far, this implementation has helped hundreds of thousands of patients receive diagnoses by first discovering what that patient likely has, then using manual methods to validate the diagnoses and treat it accordingly.

In the financial industry, many different trading platforms and programs have been developed as a result of machine learning. Through this, trades and investments are being made and managed automatically as a result of the machine learning technology. In fact, most modern trading platforms have machine learning built in where users can input certain parameters and the device will manage their trades accordingly, ensuring that they enter and exit trades at the right times. This way, they are capable of maximizing their profits and minimizing their losses in their trades.

When it comes to user behavior and the internet, machine learning has been used to make associations between things that an internet browser would likely want to view or purchase. By recognizing what their typical browsing behavior looks like, machine learning can propose new pieces of media or new objects for people to purchase through the internet based off of these recognitions.

In the financial industry again, machine learning is being used as a way to classify people. This way, banks can input certain forms of data and identify whether or not people are eligible for things like loans or credit cards, based on information such as how much they earn, what their debt to income ratio is like, or what their financial history looks like.

Machine learning is also being used to predict many different things. By looking at certain pieces of data, machine learning devices can predict things from weather to probable outcomes in businesses or even in various voting-based programs such as presidential elections. Machine learning is powerful at identifying and highlighting probable results or outcomes based on the data inputted into the machine.

Extraction is another method that can be used with machine learning. With extraction, machine learning technology can help extract web pages, articles, blogs, business reports, and emails based on certain parameters that a user uploads. For example, if you are looking for a certain piece of information out of an email you could place that in a search bar and based on smart technologies you would receive the emails that contained that information in them. In addition to helping people grow or extract things, machine learning can be used for regression. Using regression you can identify possible outcomes and optimize information by removing unnecessary information or data, or "regressing" to a point where you have a more optimized plan forward.

Chapter 2: Machine Learning Methods

When it comes to machine learning, there are four methods of machine learning that are recognized. These four methods include: supervised learning, unsupervised learning, semi-supervised learning, and reinforcement learning. Each of these methods has its own unique benefits, uses, and applications in the industry. Some people believe that the ultimate goal of machine learning is to get to the point where everything is automated, or works in a completely unsupervised manner. While this would be fascinating, the reality is that there are a lot of moral and ethical debates surrounding this idea that result in people believing that it should not be done. For that reason, the likelihood of us seeing an AI revolution where all machine learning technology is completely unsupervised is highly unlikely. Instead, it is more likely that we will see a future where there are various machine learning technologies that exist with varying levels of supervision based on their unique purpose and the sensitivity of the data they are working with.

To help you understand what each method of learning does, and to explore the moral and ethical implications of each, we are going to explore each of these four learning methods. This will help you better understand the degree to which each machine learning technology has "control" over itself, or any of the functions or systems that it operates. The more you can understand how each of these methods works, the more success you will have in understanding how machine learning can be used, what the future of it really looks like, and where different methods of application would be most beneficial.

Supervised Learning Method

The supervised learning method is comprised of a series of algorithms that build mathematical models of certain data sets that are capable of containing both inputs and the desired outputs for that particular machine. The data being inputted into the supervised learning method is known as training data, and essentially consists of training examples which contain one or more inputs and typically only one desired output. This output is known as a "supervisory signal."

In the training examples for the supervised learning method, the training example is represented by an array, also known as a vector or a feature vector, and the training data is represented by a matrix. The algorithm uses the iterative optimization of an objective function to predict the output that will be associated with new inputs. Ideally, if the supervised learning algorithm is working properly, the machine will be able to correctly determine the output for the inputs that were not a part of the training data. What this means is: the training data essentially "trains" the machine on certain parameters so that it can apply those parameters to different pieces of information in the future.

Supervised learning methods can be complete with both classification and regression algorithms. The classification algorithms can be used to create outputs that are restricted to a limited set of values, meaning that there are a limited number of "actions" that the machine could take. The regression algorithms are outputs that can have any numerical value within a specified range determined by the machine's programmer.

There is an additional area of machine learning that falls within the supervised learning method, which is called similarity learning. Similarity learning is an area where the machine learns something that overlaps with classification and regression. With this particular algorithm, the machine measures the similarity between two related objects and then "ranks" the similarity factor between multiple objects. You can easily recognize this similarity learning as something that you see in advertisements on the internet or when you are scrolling through social media.

When similarity learning has been applied, you might notice that you receive advertisements for things that would likely interest you, even if you have never actually researched them or looked them up online.

Supervised learning is a great application that can be used in conjunction with things like business, finances, and the medical system. With it, information can be accessed and retrieved without there being any implications with morals and ethics. This way, the information exists and is accessible, but we do not have to worry about it being tampered with or otherwise manipulated by the presence of a completely automated device. With supervised learning methods, everything can be interrupted by human intervention if need be. For example, if an algorithm began to show things that were too personal or too private in advertisements, the company running that advertisement company could intervene and create new parameters that ultimately prevented those results from ranking.

This way, humans can still have a fairly active level of control over the capabilities and functionality of machines.

Unsupervised Learning Method

Unsupervised learning is a set of algorithms where the only information being uploaded is inputs. The device itself, then, is responsible for grouping together and creating ideal outputs based on the data it discovers. Often, unsupervised learning algorithms have certain goals, but they are not controlled in any manner. Instead, the developers believe that they have created strong enough inputs to ultimately program the machine to create stronger results than they themselves possibly could. The idea here is that the machine is programmed to run flawlessly to the point where it can be intuitive and inventive in the most effective manner possible.

The information in the algorithms being run by unsupervised learning methods is not labeled, classified, or categorized by humans. Instead, the unsupervised algorithm rejects responding to feedback in favor of identifying commonalities in the data. It then reacts based on the presence, or absence, of such commonalities in each new piece of data that is being inputted into the machine itself.

One of the biggest applications of unsupervised learning algorithms to date comes to the field of density estimation in statistics.

Unsupervised learning has the capacity to summarize and explain data features, essentially helping data analysts gain a better understanding of various aspects of data. This way, they can develop a greater understanding of things like economics, demographics, and other statistics to create plans and strategies for whatever area of application they may be focusing on.

Semi-Supervised Learning Method

Semi-supervised is another form of a machine learning method where computers are programmed with some of the training examples missing any training labels. Still, they can be used to improve the quality of a model, allowing the device to ultimately function more effectively. Semi-supervised learning methods can range from more consistently supervised learning methods to weakly supervised learning methods. The degree to which a method is semi-supervised on this sliding scale depends on how the labels for training examples are created. In weakly supervised learning methods, the training labels are noisy, limited, or imprecise, which often helps create more effective training sets in the long run.

In more strictly semi-supervised learning methods the labels are either there, or missing, there are never labels that are incorrect or sloppy.

The goal of semi-supervised learning methods is to improve the outcomes of a device without making it completely unsupervised. This way, the device can be even more effective and complex, but is not entirely left to its own "devices," so to speak.

Reinforcement Learning Method

The reinforcement learning method is a method that is concerned with how software agents should take action in certain environments to maximize some notion of cumulative reward. Reinforcement learning is often used in game theory, operations research, control theory, information theory, multi-agent systems, stimulation-based optimization, statistics, swarm intelligence, and genetic algorithms.

For machine learning, the environment is typically represented by an "MDP" or Markov Decision Process. These algorithms do not necessarily assume knowledge, but instead are used when exact models are infeasible. In other words, they are not quite as precise or exact, but they will still serve a strong method in various applications throughout different technology systems.

The most common use of reinforcement learning is in games where there are "computer players" or a player that is represented by the computer and plays against human opponents. In these "computer players" reinforcement learning enables them to respond in a way that is not exact and precise every time, but instead in a way that actually challenges the human. This way, games cannot be memorized and overcome, but instead feature some diversity and uncertainty to them. As a result, it makes the game more enjoyable for players.

Other Learning Methods

In addition to the four aforementioned learning methods, there are some additional learning methods that are used by machine learning technology. These additional learning methods are not typically talked about as they are not significant or standard methods, but they are still important to know about. While they may not be used on a widespread basis just yet, they are being researched and may find themselves being used more and more frequently as we continue to explore and implement machine learning over time.

The additional learning methods that can be used with machine learning include: self-learning, feature learning, sparse dictionary learning, anomaly detection and association rules.

Typically, these are used in very specific areas of technology, and not in pieces of technology that are used every day by average people.

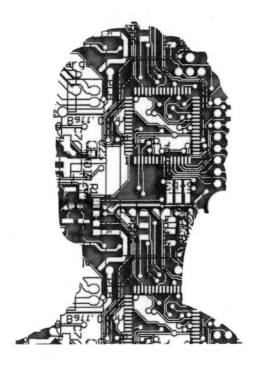

The self-learning method was introduced in 1982 and essentially means that there are no external rewards, or teacher pieces of advice.

Instead, the device is designed to be driven between cognition and emotion so that it can educate itself in a way that is meant to resemble the human brain. The device features a memory matrix that it uploads information into so that it can continue to recall previous lessons and build on them.

Feature learning is a system of several algorithms that help machine learning devices experience better representations of the inputs provided during training. These algorithms can also be called representation learning algorithms, and their goal is to preserve the information in their input while also transforming it into a method that is useful. This is completed as a pre-processing step before the device then completes a classification or prediction method.

Sparse dictionary learning means that the machine learning device is uploaded with training examples that are a linear combination of basis functions. The method itself is believed to be a spare matrix, and it is difficult to solve approximately. This particular method, although complex, has been applied in many different contexts, including classification and even image de-noising.

Anomaly detection is relevant to data mining, where anomaly detection can identify rare items, events, or other anomalies that raise suspicions because of how much they differ from the majority of the data being processed. A great example of this technology being used in today's world is in banks where the technology is used to detect and prevent fraudulent activity from taking place. Future applications might include medical screening technology where the devices can detect anomalies in DNA, or other genetic cells.

Lastly, association rule learning is a rule-based machine learning method that allows the device to discover relationships between a series of variables in large databases. In this particular learning method, the machine learning device requires "rules" to identify what relationships it is looking for so that it can bring those relationships to people's attention.

Often, the device itself will also learn new "rules" based on what it discovers, allowing new information to come to light for those monitoring the system, too. A great example of how association rule learning has been used in today's world is in the point of sale system in grocery stores. The rule that people who buy onions and potatoes are more likely to buy burgers was identified by an association rule learning method, which allowed grocers to start advertising burgers or ground meat products around the areas where they were advertising potatoes and onions, too. This way, they could improve burger sales by targeting what their audience was likely to want when shopping for onions and potatoes, too. Of course, this particular learning method can be used in many ways beyond just choosing how to sell groceries, but this is a great example.

These five additional learning methods are not the most commonly focused-on methods because they tend to be more specific, or they may be built in as "add on" methods to technology that has already been developed with a more generic method like unsupervised learning. With that being said, they are powerful and they do represent what technology is capable of, if we give it the opportunity.

Chapter 3: Big Data Analysis

Big data analysis is one of the biggest benefits that machine learning offers people who are looking to create certain outcomes with their data. For example, if you are a corporation looking to pinpoint a specific demographic within your audience that would be most likely to buy a certain product, big data analysis would be incredibly useful for you. In the past, big data analysis had to be done manually by people and it took massive amounts of time to be completed. These days, big data analysis can be done by computers, and often in a way that is far more reliable than when it is done by humans. This is because, rather than having to rely on the memory or possibly faulty organizational systems of humans, machine learning technology can rely on the technology within it to store certain pieces of information and organize it more effectively.

Virtually every machine learning device is capable of analyzing big data, and often uses this as a means for completing its required outputs. Because of how relevant big data analysis is to machine learning technology, it is important that people who are learning about machine learning take the time to learn about big data analysis, too. In this chapter we are going to discover what big data is, how it is used, and why it is so relevant and necessary in the functionality of machine learning technology.

What is Big Data?

Put simply, big data translates to extremely large sets of data that are analyzed by computers to reveal certain patterns, trends, or correlations between the information being presented in the data. Often, this data represents human behavior or interactions, either with each other or with certain objects being represented by the data. For example, this data might reflect how often certain demographics interact with each other, or it might reflect how often certain demographics interact with something such as a specific object or type of marketing strategy.

While big data in and of itself is a fairly simple term, there are countless types of data that can fall under the hat of being considered big data. For example, big data might include hundreds of thousands, or even millions, of demographic-related data, such as where people live, what age they are, and what career or education level they have.

Another type of data might include what types of illnesses people have, where those people live the most, and what type of access they have to medical care. Or, big data might include what areas of websites are being visited the most, what types of emails are opened the most, and what social media platforms are used the most. As you can see, big data can be used in many different forms of data collection, and data organizing or sorting. When it comes to collecting big data, machine learning devices can do just about anything. It can be used to identify trends and patterns, to discover anomalies, to locate certain trends and patterns that are relevant to a specific set of parameters. As you will soon find out, this can serve many purposes, from allowing the machine learning device to complete certain tasks on its own, to allow it to provide relevant information for humans to perform certain tasks. How this information is used and what the output will ultimately depend on what the device was created for, what the purpose of the big data analysis was, and how the humans running the program want to use the information.

Why is Big Data Important?

The importance of big data revolves less around how much data you have, and more around what you actually do with that data. When it comes to business, for example, you can take data from virtually any source and analyze it to discover answers that will help you improve your business in many ways.

You might be able to use this data to help you do anything from reducing costs or time in business, to developing new products or making wiser decisions that will have a better impact on your bottom line. Combining big data with high-powered analytics can help you accomplish tasks ranging from identifying the root cause of failures in business, or defects nearly the instant they happen, to detecting fraudulent behavior before it ever even affects your business. You could even use it to help generate new coupons, or improve your marketing strategies based on consumer buying habits.

Outside of business, big data can help in many ways, too. For example, in government big data can help a government identify what matters most to the people they are supporting and how they can make decisions that will improve their civilizations and societies in a meaningful way.

In schools, big data can help teachers identify where students are having the most troubles learning and implement new learning strategies to help those students learn better. In sciences big data can be used to identify certain anomalies in scientific findings to discover new patterns, or identify new areas to research or study.

Also in sciences, big data can help predict things such as new strains of illnesses, weather patterns, or certain changes that are projected to take place in various eco systems over time. There are countless ways that big data can be used to help various parts of our modern society, ranging from businesses and corporations to government and educational systems, and even sciences and beyond. Big data is important because, when used properly, it can give us the best understanding of what is going on in a certain set of analytics and what problems we may be facing. When we use this to identify problems that may cause detrimental impacts to our businesses, our societies, our eco systems, and even our bodies, this can be used to offset those impacts. As a result, we can experience a more meaningful and purposeful evolution in our businesses and societies that improves our quality of life altogether.

How is Big Data Used?

Big data is used either entirely by machine learning technology, or by humans as a way to perform a multitude of different functions. We see big data being used exclusively by machine learning technology when the technology is developed to create prediction models, or to project various different outcomes based on a series of inputs that have been made into the system. Big data can also be used exclusively by machine learning technology to produce results, such as with search engines, or to help individuals make decisions, such as with decision trees. There are countless practical applications that this type of technology can introduce, much of which we will talk about in the next section: *Applications of Big Data in Today's World.*

When it is used in conjunction with human intervention, big data can be effectively applied to many different things as well.

For example, the machine learning technology might provide an organized sequence of data that represents various analytics in such a way that humans can then take that information and turn it into a plan or a strategy to complete something. In business, for example, the machine learning technology might inform a business of the needs and interests of their consumers so that the business can go on to conceptualize a new product or service that would serve their consumers.

In this case, technology plays a vital role when it comes to big data but not so much when it comes to conceptualizing the new product or service.

Regardless of whether machine learning technology works solely on its own, or with the collaboration of humans, it can play a vital role in many different things in our modern society. From helping us resolve problems in supporting us with generating new solutions or probable outcomes, there are many ways that big data is used in today's world.

Applications of Big Data in Today's World

To help you further understand how big data can be applied, we are going to discuss practical applications of big data in today's world. In most cases, actually seeing how big data is already working with our modern world to support us in various applications is an easier way to understand what big data can actually do, why it matters, and what benefit it can offer us and our society. In today's world, we are seeing big data being used most by six different industries.

These industries include: banking, education, government, health care, manufacturing, and retail. Each of these industries is benefiting from big data in its own unique way, so we are going to discover what these methods are and why big data is so necessary to these industries.

In banking, big data is used as a way to help banks manage their customers and boost their satisfaction. Through this, banks can understand what customers' banking needs are, and how they can create new products or services that will serve their customers' banking needs.

They also use big data as a way to analyze what is going on within their systems to ensure that fraudulent activities are not taking place either from internal sources such as those who work at the bank, or external sources such as those who try to commit bank fraud. Using big data, banks can stay one step ahead of their customers, and fraudulent activity, to serve in the most effective and protected manner possible.

Big data does not just come into play in educational systems when we talk about students who are taking courses that educate them on analytics and technical analysis. Big data is also useful for educators who are looking at how they can improve school systems, support their students better, and evolve their curriculums. When an educational system is able to analyze big data, it can identify and locate at-risk students and put them in touch with helpful resources or tools that may improve their educational career. They can also help students progress at an adequate rate, and support them should they be having trouble with their progress.

In addition to helping implement new systems for students, big data can also help teachers and principals improve their own methods of teaching, while also ensuring that they are implementing the best possible methods. In other words, it can help everyone stay accountable and move toward a more effective educational system.

In health care, big data has helped things get done more quickly and accurately than ever before. From patient records and treatment plans to prescription information, big data support health care practitioners in many ways. As with the government, it is critical that the big data in the medical system is transparent, protects privacy, and meets stringent industry regulations. For that reason, while it is used, it is also a necessity that any information provided from a machine learning model is also validated by a team of specialists to ensure that they have received accurate information. This way, they are able to improve patient care and increase effectiveness in medical treatments without overlooking the ever-important aspect of ethics.

In the government, big data has been used to manage utilities, run agencies, prevent crime, and deal with traffic congestion. By using big data, they can identify what is needed, and what may not be needed, so that they can refine their management systems and have greater success in running effective systems for their society. With that being said, based on the nature of the government it is also important that they are able to address issues relating to transparency and privacy, as many are concerned that the data could be biased or botched to serve the government's preferences.

In manufacturing, big data helps boost quality control, increase output, and minimize waste associated with the manufacturing process.

In today's market, these are all highly necessary to the competitive market that products are regularly being created for and released into. In using analytics, manufacturers can actually improve the quality of their products, making them more competitive, while also making the creation process more competitive. As a result, they are often also able to reduce manufacturing costs and improve overall service. For the modern world, greener manufacturing solutions and improved quality of products are two of the most important purchasing considerations that people take into account, which means that improving these aspects can massively improve sales in companies.

Beyond manufacturing, big data can also help when it comes to retail. With big data, companies can manage and monitor customer relationships and ensure that they are ultimately building the strongest loyal following possible.

Retailers do this by identifying the best way to market to customers, discovering the most effective methods for handling transactions, and identifying the most strategic way to bring back repeat business.

In order for all of this to take place, companies track and monitor data and use this to improve their sales numbers, directly through improving relationships. Ultimately, this is how companies gauge "who" their audience is, and build their brand and mission accordingly.

Big Data Analysis Tools

There are countless different big data analysis tools that are being used to help companies track and monitor analytics in their businesses so that they can improve the quality of their customer relationships and, therefore, sales. These tools are ones that can be used by the average person, although it may be complex to use them if you are not entirely clear as to what you are doing right away. Working with the right tools is a critical opportunity for you to find ways to use analytics to help you make decisions, identify strategies, or improve outcomes based on the information you input into the system.

When we talk about big data analysis tools, what we are really talking about are types of software that can be used to compute big analysis. This software can be used on virtually any computer, making it highly accessible to just about everyone. With that being said, there are eight great big data analysis tools that anyone can start using on the market. These include: Zoho Analytics, Cloudera, Microsoft Power BI, Oracle Analytics Cloud, Pentaho Big Data Integration and Analytics, SAS Institute, Sisense, Splunk, and Tableau. To give you an understanding of how these tools use big data to support their users, we are going to explore each one in greater detail below.

Zoho Analytics

Zoho Analytics is a self-service option that's a primary focus is to help users transform large amounts of raw data into actionable reports and dashboards. They are capable of tracking business metrics, determining outliers, identifying long term trends, and discovering a multitude of hidden insights within a business. This intelligence platform is a powerful one that can transform business-oriented analytics into new strategies to help you maximize your audience and move forward in a strong manner.

Cloudera

Cloudera is a great fit for larger organizations that want to use Hadoop technology, which is an open-source framework used to store data and run applications. For this particular tool, larger organizations can create and process predictive analysis models effortlessly using several different tools that have been integrated into this unique platform. You may require the support of an IT or technical analyst to help you navigate this particular tool.

Microsoft Power BI

This particular technology has been a favorite amongst organizations for a long time, likely because the Microsoft platform is recognizable and reliable. This particular analysis platform is great for organizations that are looking for an easy way to get into analytics and leveraging analytics to help them grow their business. In addition to offering all of the analysis tools within its software, it also offers cloud based analytics and is able to perform multiple different types of data analysis and monitoring at the same time due to the way it was built.

Oracle Analytics Cloud

Oracle moved into big data analytics as a self-service company that enables companies of all sizes to leverage its platform to create different types of analytics findings from big data. The core focus of this particular tool is to ingest data and support users in finding trends, patterns, and predictive models that can support them in releasing bottlenecking and improving the quality of their company.

Pentaho Big Data Integration and Analytics

Pentaho, owned by Hitachi, is another big data analytics company. This particular company specializes in Enterprises, and is built on an open source platform. It is excellent for companies that have many varieties of data and massive data sources, meaning that they are using data in multiple ways, in multiple areas in their business, and on a large scale. Based on how it is built, it can reasonably and effortlessly handle the bigger tasks and support larger businesses, like Enterprises, in running stronger companies.

SAS Institute

SAS Institute is one of the most well-known big data tools out there because it has been around for so long. This particular company is often used for deep analytics, although it features a drag and drops functionality which means that it is extremely user friendly. With that being said, it is great for building advanced visualizations for what you want to create within your business, and can help you share that information across multiple devices. This tool can either be used locally, or in the cloud service.

Sisense

Sisense is said to be a company that makes tracking big data as easy as possible for anyone to do, no matter how new they might be to tracking big data. With its capabilities, it can support users of any size and knowledge level in getting into tracking analytics so that they can improve the quality of their companies or organizations. This particular company is excellent for larger organizations that want fast implementation time with a company that offers incredible customer service. They have a data visualization service built-in, as well as predictive modeling. This particular platform can be used on mobile or web, and can be used locally or with the cloud based service.

Splunk

Splunk is a tool that is user-friendly and web based, making it easy for many to get started with. This particular company makes it easy to collaborate with other people in your business, so if you have multiple people tracking analytics and monitoring big data you can keep all of your findings and comments local in the service.

This way, entire teams can collaborate seamlessly via the internet. This particular company is best known for creating graphs and analytic dashboards which makes tracking and presenting analytics much easier.

Tableau

Tableau is one of the top companies in the industry, and is recognized as being a great option for scientists who are known as "non-data" scientists.

It works excellent no matter what sector you are working in, and is perfect for Enterprises. This particular company uses data visualization technology, and is capable of creating data visualization without the user first needing to organize the data, which is incredibly useful. This particular platform can also help reuse existing skills to support improved big data findings so that companies can have improved analytics discoveries.

Big Data and Machine Learning

Big data and machine learning largely overlap, although they are not the same thing. Big data is a specific term referring to large categories of information that are used by software or other machine learning systems to create certain outputs. For companies and various organizations, big data is an opportunity for them to create a strong thesis around what they can do to improve the quality of their company. For machine learning, big data is frequently used to create training examples that train machine learning technology to behave in certain manners. This big data can be used to train machines to create certain outputs, to self-learn, and to complete other tasks depending on what the intention of that particular machine learning technology was designed for.

While big data and machine learning do intercept, it is important to understand that they are not actually the same thing. Big data is a pool of data on certain topics, and big data analysis is process of analyzing those pools of information for certain things. Machine learning, on the other hand, is a form of technology used to allow machines to behave in intelligent and complex manners, depending on how they were programmed and what they are intended to be used for.

Chapter 4: Machine Learning Algorithms

Machine learning technology relies on algorithms as a means to function, as algorithms are what programs these machines to perform the tasks that they were designed to perform. In some cases, these algorithms are stored on servers that are accessible by other computers through open networks such as the internet. In other cases, these algorithms are stored on servers that are accessible only through closed networks, meaning that only certain computers or devices can access the network. In either case, the algorithm is designed to make the system function in a specific manner so that it can have a certain preferred outcome. Search engines, for example, are designed with a type of machine learning algorithm that enables them to return the best possible information from the internet on any given search parameters that a user inputs into the search bar.

Search engines are not the only example of machine learning algorithms that are used with this particular form of technology, however. There are actually countless algorithms that are used to program machine learning technology so that these devices can complete their intended purposes. In addition, these algorithms are regularly being modified and improved so that they can complete different tasks all the time. Researchers are regularly looking for new algorithms and programming strategies that enable them to push the boundaries of computer sciences and program machine learning models to do new things on a regular basis.

Despite how many algorithms there are, those who are new to machine learning should focus exclusively on the models that are more relevant to beginners. These algorithms include: the K Means Clustering algorithm, artificial neural networks, decision trees, the naïve Bayes classifier algorithm, random forests, the Apriori algorithm, and linear and logistic regression. These are the most important algorithms to know about as a beginner to machine learning as they are the most commonly used, and explored, algorithms that presently make up most of the machine learning technology that we use today. As well, these are the basis for most of the new technology being developed within the machine learning industry to date.

Before we get into learning about what these algorithms are, it is important that you understand what an algorithm is in the first place and how machine learning algorithms are used.

This way, you have a stronger understanding as to how these programming methods train or program machine learning technology to function in a specific manner.

What is An Algorithm?

First things first, let's look into algorithms. Algorithms are specifically defined as: "a process or set of rules to be followed in calculations or other problem-solving operations, specifically by a computer." This definition is proposed by the Oxford American dictionary. Based on this definition, we can conclude that while most algorithms are based on computers, some algorithms are completed manually as a way to help people identify certain pieces of information or access certain pieces of knowledge. Arguably, even the rules you learned in your mathematics classes in elementary school are a form of an algorithm as they define specific rules that are to be followed during calculations. With that being said, the algorithms we are talking about with computers and machine learning models are significantly more complex than the BEDMAS technique you learned in Grade 7.

What Are Machine Learning Algorithms?

The algorithms used in machine learning ultimately program the technology or device to function in a specific manner. Essentially, the developer or programmer defines a specific set of rules and uploads that into the technology in the form of an algorithm. Following that, the device then responds in specific manners that allow the device to ultimately function in a specific manner, too. The types of algorithms being used by machine learning models closely relate to what method of learning that machine learning model is going to use. In other words, different algorithms are used in supervised machine learning methods versus unsupervised, semi-supervised machine learning algorithms, and reinforcement machine learning algorithms. These algorithms will ultimately define what the computer is meant to do, how much it is meant to do, and what outputs it is expected to create in order for it to function properly.

If a machine learning device does not produce the proper outcomes based on what the developer or programmer was looking for, one can conclude that they have created or inputted the algorithm in an incorrect manner. If this is the case, they must look through a series of complex coding to identify what the machine is doing, where it is essentially behaving "wrong," and what can be done to improve its behavior.

Once the programmer has looked through the coding, they can improve the coding to ensure that the algorithm begins behaving in the proper manner, essentially meaning that the machine learning model will begin behaving properly, too. When it comes to algorithms in machine learning models, they are always created using complex coding systems that define the rules being adhered to by that particular piece of technology. These rules define what pieces of information the technology should look for, how to authenticate and validate the quality of that information, and how to present it to the user. They also tend to define what types of inputs to look for, or other cues to look for to signal that something needs to be done.

For example, developers might program a piece of technology with "If This, Then That" or IFTTT technology so that it behaves in a specific manner. In this case, anytime a certain trigger is pulled, a specific outcome is produced. For example, if you use a search engine and type something in the search bar, it automatically pulls up results for you based on what you have searched.

Likewise, if you include certain symbols such as quotations into the search bar, it adjusts how the search parameters work and ultimately changes the results you are likely to receive based on your search terms. All algorithms in machine learning technology will always be uploaded through a system of complex codes. These codes are often written into the technology or software and then stored on servers and then distributed to other devices on a chosen network, whether that is a closed or open network.

It is very rare for the algorithm and the information relating to a software to be stored on the same platforms they are used on, as this would leave the software at risk of being infected by viruses or other malware that could disrupt the service. Instead, they tend to be stored on a remote server and are often backed up to offline devices to ensure that the original software itself is protected. This way, should anything ever happen to the machine learning system online, it could be restored by the offline backup and put back to normal in no time at all.

What is the Use of Machine Learning Algorithms?

The purpose of machine learning algorithms is ultimately to program the machines or software to do what they are meant to do. Without machine learning algorithms, the software has no way of knowing how it is supposed to behave or what it is supposed to do, which means that the user possibilities are not entirely limitless. In other words, because the machine has no way of knowing what to do, it ultimately can't do much.

With machine learning algorithms, machines can either work entirely based on what the user themselves are doing, or entirely unsupervised and on their own. This ultimately depends on what they were made to do and what the purpose of the machine itself is. A search engine software, for example, will be automatically updated but will not perform any actions unless someone using the search engine inputs information to be searched. Alternatively, a bank server that is focused on tracking transactions and detecting fraud will continue to keep track of information so long as people are using their bank services, and it functions on its own entirely in the background.

Chapter 5: K Means Clustering Algorithm

The K means clustering algorithm is one of the simplest and most popular forms of an unsupervised machine learning algorithm that exists. This particular algorithm makes it incredibly easy for developers to create, and use, machine learning technology. Because of how popular and simple this method is, it is one of the most commonly used algorithms for unsupervised machine learning methods out there. It also happens to be one of the most flexible algorithms that can create countless different outputs depending on the purpose of the machine and what the developers and programmers want it to do.

What Is the *K Means Clustering* Algorithm?

The K means clustering algorithm was designed to group similar data points together and then discover underlying patterns in those data points. The algorithm uses a fixed number of clusters in a dataset, which is represented by (k). In the case of algorithms and machine learning, clusters refer to collections of data points that are connected due to specific similarities.

Which similarities the algorithm looks for depends on what the algorithm has programmed to do, or what the developer has asked that algorithm to do. This can also be interchanged depending on the commands used and the aspect of the algorithm being interacted with. For example, let's say a large corporation was using the K means clustering algorithm about their customers so that they could improve their products and services and earn more sales.

In this case, the exact same data about customers could trigger an algorithm to point out patterns about where those customers live, what age those customers are, or what products or services they are already purchasing depending on what the developer has asked the algorithm to do.

When you are creating the K means cluster algorithm, you have to define what k means, or what target number will point to k. Once you have defined that, k will point to a number of centroids in the dataset, or the imaginary or real location that is used to represent the center of a cluster of data.

How Does This Algorithm Work?

The K means algorithm processes learning data through mining data by first identifying an initial group of randomly selected centroids. These are then used as the beginner points for every cluster made. From there, the K means algorithm will perform repetitive calculations to optimize the positions of the centroids, ensuring that they are as accurate as possible. It will continue doing this until a specific set of parameters are met that indicate that it is time to stop.

The specific parameters that will stop a K means algorithm, ultimately meaning it has found it's "destination," are simple. There are two things that can happen that will stop the calculations from taking place and ultimately define the end destination of the K means algorithm. The process will stop when one of these two parameters is met, and does not require for both of them to be present in order to work.

The first parameter that could be met in order to stop the calculation and optimization of clusters is if the centroids have stabilized.

This essentially means that there is no more change in their values because the process was successful and there was no need for it to continue. In other words, the calculations are no longer finding more optimal centroids, meaning that there is nothing more for it to do. In this case, it outputs its findings of the centroids for the user to then identify what those findings are and use them in whatever way they needed to. This particular parameter can only be met if the centroids have a specific, finite centroid that is exact and measurable. In this case, it can be located and presented to the user.

The second parameter that the K means cluster algorithm could reach that would prevent it from conducting any further calculations is if the defined number of repetitions has been achieved. In this parameter, the developer has to decide how many times the algorithm is going to perform the calculations to optimize its findings and produce the results. The more times the calculation is done, the more accurate the centroid will be. The fewer times the calculation is done, the less accurate the centroid will be.

This particular parameter is used when no clear centroid exists and so the programmer or developer wants to encourage the algorithm to locate the most accurate centroid possible. If the developer were to decide that they needed a more accurate centroid, they could increase the number of times the calculation was repeated to ensure that they had the best possible results.

Based on the nature of the K means algorithm, those using this particular algorithm do not need to upload data into specific classifications but instead can use centroids to encourage the algorithm to identify these classifications on its own.

Since the algorithm is unsupervised, the goal is that it will classify the datasets into the best sets possible based on what you need the algorithm to do, ultimately allowing it to provide the most accurate results possible.

The final pieces of information outputted by the K means algorithm are referred to as final classifications or clusters of data, which means that it is ultimately the most complete and accurate set of data based on what you have asked the algorithm to do.

Ideally, it should take the initially anonymous data points and turn them into something that is complete with their own classifications and identities that represent patterns and trends within the data that was inputted in the first place.

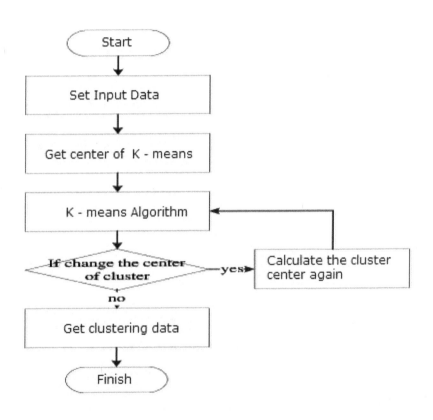

When Should This Algorithm be Used?

The K means clustering algorithm can be used in multiple different settings, ranging from behavioral segmentation to inventory categorization, and more. Because of how flexible this algorithm is, it can be applied to a variety of different uses, all of which can be incredibly helpful across various industries.

The five most common areas that the K means cluster algorithm is used include: behavioral segmentation, inventory categorization, sorting sensor measurements, detecting bots or anomalies, and tracking and monitoring classification change. This can be beneficial to many industries, making it useful in all sorts of machine learning technologies and networks. To help you better understand these practical applications and uses, we are going to explore these five different areas of application in greater detail so that you can get a better idea of what the K means clustering algorithm actually does for them.

Behavioral Segmentation

Behavioral segmentation studies the behavior of different people. When it comes to the K means clustering algorithm, companies are able to get complete behavioral profiles on their customers that enable them to understand how they can better serve those customers. From an ethical point of view, this information can be used to shape a more enjoyable relationship between the customer and the business, ultimately creating more successful business, too.

This can also be used to identify new products or services that could be introduced, or old ones that could be revamped, to improve a customer's experience with a given business. In addition to behavioral segmentation supporting the segmentation of customers based on purchase history, it can also support businesses in segmenting things like activities on websites, applications, or even specific platforms. For example, if a company were to launch a new app to support customers in shopping with their brand, it could segment where the app was being used the most, how, by who, and when.

Another way that behavioral segmentation has been used with the K means clustering algorithm is to define personas based on interests. In the analytical world, this is called *psychological profiling* and means that you use analytics to identify which types of people are most likely to behave in certain ways. Rather than attempting to come up with and confirm your theories through your own research, you could use the K means clustering algorithm to create clear and accurate psychological profiles. Through this, you could use these psychological profiles to identify which are most active in your business, and which could become more active in your business if they had the right products or services available to them. Beyond just business, these psychological profiles can also help identify information relevant to the educational system, or even the government. With them in hand, educational programs can identify high risk students and offer them more support, or the government could use these profiles to identify what types of organizations or support programs may be useful to their public.

Lastly, profiles can also be made based on activity monitoring, rather than interests. Often, true psychological profiles created through analytics will feature both interest monitoring and activity monitoring to create a clearer understanding as to who is being represented by the profile. In some cases, however, these two metrics may be looked at separately for different means. For example, interest-based personas could be used to identify what types of products to advertise to certain people, whereas activity based monitoring could identify where to advertise those things to create the largest amount of interaction with that advertisement.

Inventory Categorization

When it comes to inventory categorization, larger corporations and those that have hundreds of thousands or even millions of products can benefit from learning how to categorize their products more effectively. Proper inventory categorization methods ensure that inventory stays organized, that companies know what is in stock and what is not, and that inventory is managed properly. For example, a proper management system can ensure that if a company has 10,000 units of a certain product, the units are evenly distributed across their 50 locations, rather than all sent to one or two single locations.

With the K means clustering algorithm, the algorithm can categorize inventory based on sales activity, and based on manufacturing metrics. This means that the inventory can be categorized based on just about any set of predetermined categories the company may want to put in place. On a website, for example, the company can use the K means clustering method to organize their products based on best sellers, most relevant, top rated, or most cost effective. In their private inventory management systems, they may organize them based on their SKU, which would be a series of numbers used to identify what the product is and what category of products it belonged to. For example, the SKU might reflect that the product is a video game, or a small appliance.

By using these proper inventory category management systems, thousands of pieces of inventory can be uploaded and managed at the moment noticed using the K means clustering algorithm. For businesses, this can mean more effective inventory management for their employees, as well as easier shopping experiences for their customers. In both scenarios, the algorithm has effectively supported them by creating more success in their sales.

Sorting Sensor Measurements

There are multiple different types of sensors that may be monitored or tracked using the K means clustering algorithm. For example, it may be used to detect activity types in motion sensors, allowing the sensor to identify when something has come into the radar of the motion sensor. In some cases, it may be very basic and simply detect any motion. In other cases, it may detect certain amounts of motion, frequencies of motion, or types of motion and exclude other forms of motion.

As a result, it is able to provide feedback on the specific type of motion and possibly even be used as the basis to build other more complex motion sensor-based projects off of. For example, the K means clustering algorithm might recognize a certain type of motion and then send off a signal to a security device to inform the owner of that device that something suspicious has been detected by the motion sensor. While the trigger and following behaviors would not be the responsibility of the K means clustering algorithm, the detection of the motion that initially indicated the trigger was met would be. Another thing it can do is detect and group images. Using proper algorithm measurements, the K means clustering algorithm can detect certain features in an image and present them upon request.

For example, you would be able to upload 10,000 random pictures into the algorithm and it would group pictures together based on similar features. All images featuring the Eiffel Tower, for example, would be grouped together. Likewise, all images featuring people, or even a certain person, would be grouped together.

In present day, this exact technology is recognized in modern smart phones where people can open their Photo Applications and type in a keyword, thus causing the phone to show any photographs they may have taken that featured that keyword. For example, if you were to open up your photo application and type in "Dog," if you had taken any photographs of a dog with your device, the device would show you all of those photographs. In addition to being able to group photographs, the K means clustering algorithm can also group and separate audio.

This means it can be used to separate audio tracks to draw out specific instruments or voices, or even categorize audio tracks based on certain types of sounds that are present in that audio track. This is particularly helpful, for example, in cases where investigators may be trying to understand what someone is saying but is incapable of hearing their voice due to background noise in a certain audio tape. Using the K means clustering algorithm, they can separate the audio and remove background noise, making it easier for people to hear the actual voice being represented on that particular audio track.

Another way that sorting sensor measurement is completed using the K means clustering algorithm is to identify groups in health monitoring. In this case, an individual might receive a series of different tests and measurements to track their health, and then they would go on to input that into the algorithm.

From there, the machine learning technology would be able to recognize normal patterns in their health, and identify any possible anomalies or differences in their health patterns. This way, they could accurately keep track of their health and quickly recognize anything was different from what it should be.

Detecting Bots or Anomalies

Aside from detecting anomalies in health, the K means clustering algorithm can also detect bots and anomalies in computers and software. This means that the algorithm can detect anytime bot activity is suspected in a certain application and can warn the application authorities of it, or shut down the activity if the device or software has been given the instruction to do so. A great example of this is commonly seen on social media, where many accounts will use bots to attempt to build followers and increase activity and engagement on their profiles.

On the day of the influencer, this is seen as an opportunity to rapidly build your popularity and increase your engagement so that you are more likely to land brand deals and earn an income from your business. Typically, most social media platforms frown upon bot use however as it can dilute the quality of the platform and make the experience less enjoyable for other users. As a result, they tend to monitor for and ban anyone who has been suspected of using bots.

In order to identify when and where bots are being used, rather than attempting to employ thousands of people to monitor the platform, they instead use the K means clustering algorithm to effectively remove, or suspend, the offending accounts.

Aside from detecting bots, the K means clustering algorithm has also been used to monitor activity on networks to make sure that nothing separate from the network itself has hacked the system in an unauthorized and unlawful manner. By setting up the algorithm to monitor activity, it is capable of recognizing anytime someone has attempted to hack into or attach itself to the network so that it can eliminate their advances. The algorithm is generally set up to automatically deny access for outliers so that their systems cannot be hacked or disrupted by those who are attempting to maliciously interrupt the network itself. This way, rather than having to manually protect their network there is a complex algorithm in place taking care of it.

Tracking and Monitoring Classification Change

Another way that the K means clustering algorithm can support developers and programmers is through detecting changes in where data is placed over time. For example, if a certain piece of data groups effectively with one classification, but over time groups more effectively with another classification, this can be monitored through the K means clustering algorithm.

An example of this would be if, say, a certain demographic was largely buying name brand from a store but then began buying less known but more eco-friendly brands over time, this would be detected by the algorithm. In this particular instance, this change would represent the fact that more people preferred eco-friendly brands, and would indicate to that company that they should focus on purchasing and selling more eco-friendly brands in the future.

This particular tracking and monitoring of data changing from one classification to another can serve in many ways when it comes to tracking data. It can help track the evolution and change of people, or certain experiences, creating a more rounded understanding of various classifications for humans. In this case, you would be able to effectively create an understanding of your customers and use this knowledge to create more meaningful programs, products, services, offerings, marketing, or other developments for those individuals.

Beyond tracking evolution, this particular area of the K means clustering algorithm can also help track devolution, or areas where regression or negative changes have developed in a system. For example, let's say you are tracking the wellbeing of a community, if you recognized that a certain group of society was beginning to experience a negative impact from the present societal structure, you could use this to help with advancements. This could, say, lead to the development of new social programs that would support the society in a more meaningful manner, helping everyone have access to equal rights and support from that particular segment of society.

Chapter 6: Artificial Neural Networks

Artificial neural networks are also known as connectionist systems, and they are a form of computing systems that are inspired by biological neural networks, such as the ones found in humans and other animal species. With that being said, they are not identical to biological neural networks because a biological neural network is more complex in nature, and would be incredibly difficult to reproduce in the form of coding or computing technology.

The purpose of the artificial neural network is to "learn" how to perform tasks by using examples as a means to "understand" how a task should be completed. Typically, the artificial neural network is not actually programmed with task-specific rules, but instead is shown examples of what it is expected to do and then, based on how it is developed and programmed, learns how to do these tasks on its own.

Artificial neural networks became incredibly popular in the mid-1900s and were developed upon over time by computer scientists who were fascinated by how these artificial neural networks could allow computers to learn and function. They became the basis for many different advanced computing technologies at the time, and served a massive purpose in helping to increase the capacity of computers, mainly through the tasks that could be accomplished through a computer device. Over the years, the artificial neural network has been improved upon over and over again, until the point where they are now some of the most powerful forms of computer there is out there.

As a result of all of this development, artificial neural networks have rapidly approached human-like capacities ranging from handwriting recognition to learning about languages and other tasks that are often reserved for human practice.

Artificial neural networks are likely to be the basis for any form of artificial intelligence that represents the form of robots that people frequently think about when they consider a robotic "species."

For example, a robot that had human-like qualities both in appearance and in functionality. If a robot ever were to be developed in this capacity, it is likely that it would be programmed with the support of artificial neural networks.

What Are *Artificial Neural Networks?*

As previously mentioned, artificial neural networks are a computerized model of biological neural networks, although they do not quite look the same or behave entirely the same. In a sense, artificial neural networks are a more devolved version of the biological neural network that makes your, and my, brain work. The development of the artificial neural network has allowed for it to "learn" on its own, based on a series of information or examples that have been fed to it. For example, an artificial neural network could engage in image recognition and begin to identify a common thing in the image, such as "cat." This could be trained to the artificial neural network by uploading a series of images and labeling them as either "cat" or "no cat." The artificial neural network would then be able to identify what the cats actually were based on all of the examples in the pictures. Through that, they would be able to identify cats in the future.

When this is accomplished, the neural network has no prior knowledge of what cats are, meaning that they have no idea that cats have fur, tails, whiskers, or faces that look like cats. In other words, the device has no means of identifying what a cat is, other than by processing all of the example images and formulating its own consensus. When the artificial neural network is properly developed, it creates the proper consensus in virtually all circumstances, making it an incredibly advanced and impressive algorithm.

The purpose of the artificial neural network is to solve problems using the exact same methods that the human brain would. With that being said, over time the focus of the development was largely based on advancing these artificial neural networks to be able to perform very specific tasks, like engaging in computer vision or speech recognition, or even filtering social networks or playing video games. Some have even been developed to engage in medical diagnosis, or to paint pictures. As a result, they have deviated further away from true biological neural networks and into ones that are specialized to perform specific tasks with incredible accuracy.

How Does They Work?

An artificial neural network is developed with a collection of connected units, or nodes, which are correctly referred to as artificial neurons. Despite having the same term as biological neurons, and being loosely developed based off of biological neurons, these neurons do not behave the same way that a biological neuron does. Instead, they carry certain pieces of information and then connect to other neurons in a way to formulate entire behaviors. In a biological brain, these connections would be called synapses, and this is essentially the same thing that the artificial neurons do. In the artificial neuron network, the nodes are designed to transmit information between each other based on what that information is and what it means. Through a complex algorithm, this then becomes an "understanding" of the information being fed to the system, which results in human-like thoughts and behavioral patterns. With that being said, most artificial neural networks are incapable of passing true emotion or sentient energy back and forth through their nodes, which means that they will behave differently from how a human would actually behave.

Artificial neurons in the artificial neural network are each coded with real numbers, rather than biological information. Through that, they also have what have known edges, which is where they connect with each other and transmit information back and forth between other artificial neurons.

Neurons and their edges have what are known as weights, which are specific numerical values that measure the capacity of that neuron. Over the learning process, these weights adjust to reflect increased information being learned through the network. Each neuron will have a threshold, and if that threshold is met it will no longer be able to engage in the learning process.

If this occurs, the artificial neural network will then begin to attempt to work together with other artificial neurons to complete the same task. If it runs out of other artificial neurons to connect with, the process stops and the machine has "reached capacity." Another form of artificial neuron thresholds is represented by neurons being coded to only receive certain forms of information. By only being able to receive certain forms of information, the artificial neural network is able to organize which nodes are involved in various tasks, allowing it to keep itself organized and functional.

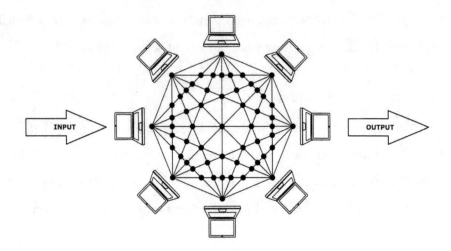

At this point, there are many different types of artificial neural networks that are being used for different reasons. The simplest forms of artificial neural networks use more static components, such as having a limited number of units, layers, unit weights, and topology.

Other more dynamic artificial neural networks allow for these areas to develop in a more intentional capacity so that they can evolve through the learning process and become more complex. The latter form of an artificial neural network is more complicated and takes significantly longer to design, however it does make the learning process shorter as the device is already smarter from square one.

As a result, it is able to learn faster and perform its intended functions with greater ease. The former variety of artificial neural networks is less complicated and is much easier to build, however it also takes significantly longer to train it anything, meaning that the learning process can be lengthy and even delayed in some cases.

In addition to the complexity of the machine varying, there are also varying degrees of supervision involved in artificial neural networks. Because of how complex they are and what they are capable of accomplishing, they have largely been developed with more supervision being required by the operator to ensure that learning is being done in the proper intended manner. This way, the machine learns what it is meant to learn and functions as it should, and it is not capable of doing anything it was not designed to do. In other artificial neural networks, however, they have been completely designed to run independently so that they do not require any significant human intervention. In these particular artificial neural networks, just about anything goes and they can be used in any number of ways.

When Should They be Used?

When it comes to artificial neural networks, a lot of people argue the ethics around them. This is particularly common in people who do not clearly understand how they are used, or those who are afraid that they will be built into machines that are capable of learning how to turn against mankind and become dangerous, essentially. Naturally, these types of fears and concerns are valid but should not be worried about too much as modern artificial intelligence and artificial neural networks are far from being able to do anything significant on their own. Although they are incredibly powerful and functioning "brains," most lack proper bodies or other extremities to be able to actually perform anything. At this point, there is still a long way to go before we have completely functional artificial neural networks that feature both the smarts of present-day networks and the capacity of a robot with properly mobile and functioning extremities.

With that being said, artificial neural networks are still being used in a massive way in today's world.

Since their conception, they have been a focal point for many computer scientists and researchers, and as such there have been many tasks that have been able to be performed by these unique and diverse networks. In fact, you might be surprised to realize just how far this technology has already come, and what it is capable of achieving. The current areas where artificial neural networks are being used the most include: identification and process control, general game playing, various forms of recognition, 3D reconstruction, diagnosis, finances, and filtering.

Identification and Process Control

Identification and control, and process control, is an incredible feature of the artificial neural networks. Certain developments have led to these networks being able to essentially recognize specific systems and begin to actually control those systems purposefully. A great example of this is with vehicle control, where vehicles are able to become self-driving, or are able to monitor certain "behaviors" and support the driver accordingly.

For example, these days many modern vehicles are able to apply the brakes before the driver were to hit something, such as a pedestrian or an unexpected obstacle in the road. While these systems are still largely debated and are still in the process of being developed to become more effective and efficient, they are starting to make their way into circulation to be used by cars in a more broad manner.

General Game Playing

Game playing has been completed by artificial neural networks in many ways, too. This goes for both physical forms of game play, and virtual forms of game play. To date, machines have been trained to play games like chess or checkers flawlessly, often beating their opponents by a landslide, or serving as a formidable and strong opponent that poses a real challenge for the individual playing against the network. These designs have been made to either interpret knowledge and request the support of a human to move the piece for them, or with a robotic arm that allows the artificial network to both make decisions about game play and then complete the move on their own.

Outside of actual real world game play, artificial neural networks have also been used to help design digital game play systems, too. These artificial neural networks are able to be hooked up to a game playing device and are able to play digital games, such as on X Box or PlayStation by essentially "watching" the screen and playing just as a real human player would.

In both cases, these artificial neural networks have proven to be incredibly quick at learning about new techniques and practices so that they can effectively play the games that they have been developed to play. The more effective a machine is developed, the more success it has in playing the game, too, which results in even more success down the line since it is essentially learning as it goes. Eventually, these machines can become so powerful that they are nearly impossible for any average human to beat in the games that they were designed to play.

Various Forms of Recognition

Artificial neural networks are incredibly skilled when it comes to varying forms of recognition. From recognizing faces and voices, to recognizing gestures and even handwriting, they are incredibly powerful. Some have even been designed to recognize what text says and then act based on the text that it has "read." In addition to these forms of recognition, they can also recognize various patterns, either in codes, data, or even in signals being gestured to the device.

For example, if a specific sequence of signals were given to a trained machine, it would be able to perform specific tasks based on what those signals were developed to mean for that device. Recognition helps these devices in becoming aware of and informing other complex parts of their systems to complete certain functions.

Through this recognition it can begin to classify pieces of information within its own system and then use that information to inform other parts of the technology to complete certain tasks. At this rate, however, the artificial neural networks' involvement would be exclusive to the "thinking" or the receiving information, classifying it, and then outputting specific signals through the rest of the artificial neural network. Any tasks that were completed afterward, such as triggering movement in a robotic extremity, would be part of a different programming feature that was triggered into action based on what the artificial neural network "said."

3D Reconstruction

3D reconstruction means that a computer can capture the shape and appearance of real objects and then, if it wants, change the shape in time so that it can be "reconstructed." The purpose of this is typical to improve the structure of something, such as when it comes to design or even with medical imaging. Based on the advancements of artificial neural networks, these systems are actually able to aid the process 3D reconstruction massively. As a result, they are known as being fundamental in the process of 3D reconstruction.

Diagnosis

Based on how they work, artificial neural networks have the capacity to engage in medical diagnosis. Through this, the ethical standards say that these devices can be used to formulate a diagnosis, but humans must validate that diagnosis using manual tests to ensure that the device was correct and the diagnosis is accurate. With that being said, artificial neural networks have been used to diagnose varying types of cancers, ranging from lung cancer to prostate cancer, and it can even distinguish cancerous cells from healthy or typical cells.

Finances

In finances, various computer scientists have been developing artificial neural networks that can engage in tasks such as automated trading systems. This is how various high tech traders are able to engage in consistent trades, even if they are not actively engaging in any trading activity themselves. As a result, they are able to essentially earn passive money through the stock market, or other trading platforms, without any human intervention.

As well, when cryptocurrency was first introduced, many computer scientists formed artificial neural networks to mine for the cryptocurrency so that they could begin to collect these currencies. As a result, they were able to take part in one of the world's first cryptocurrency experiments, and many of them made massive money doing it.

Filtering

Artificial neural networks are frequently used in social networks and emails as a way to conduct spam filtering, amongst other forms of filtering. Based on how they are developed, these networks are able to identify varying forms of information from what is being uploaded to social networks, or sent out via. emails, and classify accordingly. When it comes to email spam filtering, this is done in a relatively simple manner. The artificial neural network merely "reads" the emails and determines what is spam, and what is not spam. Of course, humans can always override the reading and change an email's label if they find that the filter did not function appropriately, or that an email made it into the wrong label.

For social networks, the functionality of this is more complex. Rather than simply deeming what is spam and what is not, these artificial neural networks can do a lot. They can detect and take down photos featuring certain types of graphics that are not permitted on social networks, such as nudity or violence. They can also apply filters over particularly graphic and possibly offensive images to ensure that people are not automatically being exposed to photographs that may be too graphic or violent for them to see. As well, they can recognize when someone may be posting something that indicates that they or someone else is in danger and it can offer support measures to assist them in hopefully protecting themselves and getting out of danger. These filters can also do basic spam filtering to prevent spam from making it onto the platforms, or identify and remove bots to ensure that they are not taking over networks.

Artificial neural networks are clearly incredibly advanced forms of technology that can help take machine learning to a whole new level. Many people think that the future of artificial neural networks lies in developing complete robots that are far more advanced and complex than existing ones. For example, developing an entire robotic species that ultimately functions and behaves on its own. Of course, there are many ethical considerations we have to take into account, and other things that need to be addressed before this happens. However, the reality of a world where robots are far more prominent in our society is likely not as far off as many people think, and they could be used to bring about a revolution that completely changes life as we know it.

Chapter 7: Decision Trees

Decision trees are a form of visualization algorithm. What this means is that they take certain pieces of information and organize them in specific classifications, completing their intended functions as necessary. However, the process used by the algorithm is visually displayed in a way that makes it easy for the human mind to follow along and witness what was completed during the algorithm process. What ends up happening is we are shown statistical data in a way that makes sense, that shows us how certain conclusions were drawn, and that helps us use these conclusions to formulate decisions or make new plans or strategies going forward. That is exactly the goal of decision trees, with the entire focus largely being around how decisions were made and what was considered in the process of the decision being made.

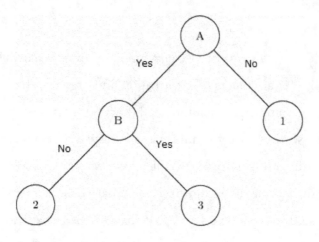

Decision trees largely show like a flow-chart, although they are an official form of machine learning algorithm that serves a very specific purpose when it comes to how and why they are used in various machine learning technology. In this chapter we are going to discover exactly what a decision tree is, how it works, and when it is used so that you can understand this unique decision making algorithm and what benefit it serves in machine learning. Because of how niche it is, it is one that definitely serves a strong, and very specific purpose.

What Are *Decision Trees*?

Decision trees are a tool that uses a tree shaped graph to support individuals or organizations in making decisions. Using a decision tree you can identify possible consequences of your decision, as well as chance event outcomes, utility, and even resource costs. When it comes to making large decisions in big corporations especially, decision trees are an excellent way to identify exact areas where growth will prove to be most valuable and where companies will be able to get the most benefit from growth. However, they can also be used in many other ways.

The decision tree is always shown in a flowchart style structure which shows the individual running the decision what things have been considered, what the possible outcomes are, as well as what the probable outcomes are. These flowcharts are made based on the fact that life is a complex thing and there is no way to guarantee what is going to happen, or how it is going to happen. With that being said, using laws of probability and various calculations, the decision tree algorithm can identify what is most likely to happen given a certain set of circumstances, or certain situations.

When you look at a decision tree, each branch of the tree represents a specific outcome of the test. Then, each leaf node, or "end" of the branch represents a class label. In order for a class label to be reached, a decision must move from the root node (the initial decision) through the branches (possible outcomes) and into the leaf nodes (final outcomes.)

This process takes place through various classification rules that determine what will likely happen and how this information would be most accurately categorized on the decision tree. Everything is based on an algorithm and calculations that measure probability to ensure that the tree is as close to accurate as possible. Barring an incredibly unexpected and untraceable external event that could completely change the decision being made, this tree is typically incredibly accurate and can reliably be followed by those watching it.

When it comes to machine learning algorithms, the decision tree is one of the most popular supervised algorithms that is used. These algorithms can support predictive models with high accuracy, and can make it easy to stabilize and interpret results to ensure that you are taking appropriate action based on the decision you have made, or need to make. Unlike linear models that point down one clear path toward a specific outcome, decision trees represent all possible outcomes and are incredibly adaptable. Through this, virtually any kind of problem can be solved using a decision tree, as they can be used to show you so much information. As well, if you find that part way through the process you need to change direction, you can refer back to your decision tree to identify how you could change direction and what the probable outcome of a changed direction would be.

The algorithm within decision trees that results in them being non-linear and exhaustive is called "Classification and Regression Trees" or CART. This particular algorithm is used in decision trees, as well as other non-linear models that are used by machine learning algorithms.

This can include regression trees, a random forest which we will talk about later, gradient boosting, and of course decision trees.

How Do *Decision Trees* Work?

Decision trees are commonly used in solving data science problems, such as what should be done to resolve certain troubles that a scientist is facing. This could include anything from identifying possible outcomes of certain medical treatments, to identifying possible outcomes of certain marketing strategies or even initiatives that organizations or governments might take to attempt to improve the state of something. Decision trees are said to be far more effective than any other decision making a process out there because they can calculate massive amounts of big data and turn up complete, accurate results that let people or organizations know how to proceed.

Decision trees are something that we can do in our own brains, to one degree or another. When we are completing a decision tree in our minds, we are essentially looking at a problem and considering all of the possible solutions and what those solutions would entail.

You have likely done this yourself, and some people even find themselves doing it to the point where it almost becomes obsessive because they are trying to make sure that they make the right decision. With that being said, the trouble of a mental decision tree is that you are not able to actually represent that tree in a visual manner that shows you what truly is likely to happen, and what the possible outcomes would be. Furthermore, your brain is ridden with biases and limitations that prevent it from being able to truly recognize every single possible outcome, as well as the probability of those outcomes coming to fruition.

With a decision tree, the information is carefully calculated using a specific algorithm that essentially guarantees that the information is sound and true. This way, you can feel confident that the results you gain from the decision tree are likely to be accurate and that you can safely follow them and expect that the probable outcome you anticipated based on the results of the tree will, in fact, be the actual result you experience, too.

On the decision tree, there are seven things you need to know about. These include: the root node, splitting, the decision node, the leaf node, pruning, branches, and parent and child nodes. Each of these nodes represents a specific part of the tree, and learning how they work will inform you as to how the algorithm reads and presents information, and how you can read the decision tree to make your conclusions and choices going forward.

The Root Node

The root node is the initial node at the very top of the decision tree. This node represents the entire population of the tree under it, meaning that this is ultimately the first layer of knowledge being fed into the tree. Typically, the root node represents the primary decision that the person needs to make, and the topic of that particular decision.

Splitting

Splitting is the term used to describe the process of one node splitting into two or more nodes. As the tree drops down into further classifications of information, ultimately leading it to a decision, it splits up nodes into several smaller nodes that represent different pieces of information. All of these pieces of information will, in one way or another, be relevant to the topic and the decision being made.

The Decision Node

Decision nodes are any nodes that have nodes splitting off of them. These represent a new decision that needs to be made in order for different outcomes to be created. These decisions are sub-decisions of the primary decision, but they all lead toward an outcome that is relevant to the primary decision that needs to be made. For example, let's say the primary decision is: "Should I eat a sandwich for dinner?" this would become a decision node when the node split and two smaller nodes were made that said "Yes" or "No." If those smaller nodes were to break out into more smaller nodes through the splitting process, they would become decision nodes, too.

The Leaf Node

Leaf nodes are nodes where they do not split off. These are the "final outcome" of a decision tree, and represent what would happen if you made all of the decisions up until that point based off of the tree. These show you, ultimately, what to expect if you act based on the trees algorithm and what it has suggested for you to do. If you find yourself at a leaf node, you can consider your decision and all subsequent decisions complete, and that particular experience would then be brought to closure since no further decisions or actions could possibly be taken.

Pruning

Pruning occurs when people choose to remove sub-nodes of a decision node. Sometimes, the decision nodes will represent something that the person or organization making the decision would never do. Sometimes these may be irrelevant, unreasonable, impossible, or unethical and so right from the start the individual or organization knows that they will not be taking action based on those decisions.

In order to clean up the tree and make it more readable, and useful, they will do what is called "pruning." This essentially means that they remove the decision nodes so that only decisions they would reasonably take are reflected on the tree. In a sense, you can see this as being the opposite of splitting.

Branches

Branches are subsections of the entire tree. So, let's say that your primary decision splits off into four decisions, each of which splits off into several smaller decisions. Those four decisions would then become "branches" as they represent different completely different subsections based on an action that you could take, and the possible outcomes that you would face if you took those actions.

Parent and Child Nodes

Parent and child nodes are simply a way of representing larger decision nodes versus smaller decision nodes. The parent node is one that is higher up on the tree, directly above the smaller node in question. The child node, then, is the one lower down on the tree, directly below the larger node in question. Child nodes can go down several "generations," but in order to be related to the parent node, they must directly draw back to that specific decision at some point when you are drawing your way back up the tree.

How the Tree Works

When the algorithm is processed and information, such as the primary decision, is inputted into the algorithm, the decision tree goes on to fill out all of the nodes and branches based on the information you have inputted into the system. This is all automatically done through the algorithm based on any information you have fed the system at the time of creating your tree.

If you have any situations, circumstances, or other things to factor in or consider, you would want to write those down in your algorithm to ensure that they are accounted for upon the creation of the tree. Once the tree was created, you could look through the decisions and prune the tree to remove any decisions that you absolutely know you would not make.

For example, if they require you to do something impossible, unreasonable, irrelevant, or unethical, you could prune those branches away so that the tree more clearly represented things that you would actually do.

How the Tree is Read

After the decision tree is complete, you would look through the tree starting at the root decision. Then, you would look at your desired outcome. From there, you would draw your way from the root to the desired decision and identify what choices would need to be made and considerations would need to be factored in for you to be able to reach your ideal outcome.

If you find that the method is something you would not, or could not, do you can always read the tree differently. In this case, rather than reading from the bottom up, you could read from the top down. Reading from the top down would require you to look at your initial decision, and ultimately pick your path down the tree based on what is most likely, or most possible. As a result, you would find your way to your probable outcome based on the decisions that you have made.

After you have successfully read the decision tree, you need to turn your findings into a strategy or a plan for how you will proceed and create your desired outcome. All of your decisions in your strategy or plan should be based on the findings of the decision tree so that you are able to create the outcome you desire to create. This way, you are more likely to have the desired outcome, and you are able to take the clearest path possible. Ideally, you should look at the path that is going to get you to where you want to go with the least amount of steps. This expedites your results and ensures that you are not wasting time, energy, or resources on different steps that are not relevant for you to be able to create your desired outcome. The more direct your path to your desired outcome is, the more success you will likely have with the decision and the tree you have made.

When Should *Decision Trees* be Used?

Decision trees are frequently used in business decisions, government decisions, educational decisions, and other decisions within large organizations. It can also be used in data sciences, specifically around computer programming, to identify what possible functions a programmed device could feature. In each area of application, the use of the decision tree is the same and the benefit is the same, however the way that it is created and the information it features will vary from tree to tree.

Let's take a deeper look at how they can be applied to give you an understanding as to what a decision tree can do in practical application.

Business Decisions

Decision trees are frequently used in business decisions, especially within larger organizations where there are so many moving parts and so many pieces of data and information to consider. Typically, decision trees will be used to help businesses create certain decisions in terms of marketing, product development, or expansion, to identify areas where they can increase business productivity and, therefore, increase revenue, too. The goal is always to identify expected and unexpected means of growth so that companies are more likely to take the best route toward growth possible. Naturally, growth and increased revenue is always the goal with businesses.

When using decision trees, businesses can factor in everything from income, budgets, customer relationships and retention, new customer acquisition, employees, and even external factors like economics and location when it comes to making decisions. By being able to introduce so many different focuses on the classification system, businesses can get accurate representations of what ideas would be best for them based off of the decisions shown in the decision tree.

Government Decisions

In government, decision trees can be used as a means to determine how a government can improve areas of their society while being able to reasonably consider factors such as the people they are leading, their budget, and the resources they have to help them.

As a result, they can find rational, reasonable, and effective solutions to problems like funding, providing enough resources for their public, and more. When used effectively, a government can use decision trees to make the best choices for their people so that they can become effective and meaningful leaders.

Educational Decisions

In educational programs, decision trees can be used to determine how budgets will be spent, what types of information should be included in curriculums, and what new resources or services could be offered to support student learning.

Through factoring in things such as budget, students, learning comprehension, faculty, and resources, education boards can discover ways to overcome challenges being presented to their school system and improve results for their staff and students.

Programming Decisions

In programming, decision trees can be used to help programmers identify what route would be the most effective and direct way for them to program a certain piece of technology. When it comes to programming and developing new technology, creating the most direct route to your goal is important as it ensures that your goal is met and that there are not so many things that could go wrong with the goal you have. The more effectively you can choose the right algorithm or programming measure, the more effective you will be in creating a clear cut path toward your goal and programming your device effectively. This way, there is no "filler" code that could increase risk by presenting the opportunity for the code to break or malfunction, possibly rendering the entire coding network useless for that particular device.

Decision trees definitely have a strong capacity to support people in the technology industry, as well as in data sciences, when it comes to making rational and sound decisions.

By using decision trees, individuals and organizations can ensure that they have exhausted all of their possibilities and that through that they are taking the best possible steps forward to reach their goals and resolve any possible problems that have risen along the way.

Chapter 8: Naïve Bayes Classifier Algorithm

The naïve Bayes classifier is an algorithm that is considered to be incredibly basic and that, like the decision tree, has a very niche focus on what it is meant to do when it comes to machine learning. This particular algorithm uses simple probabilistic classifiers to perform functions such as filtering spam versus legitimate content, or other similar functions.

When it comes to the naïve Bayes classifier, there is actually not one single algorithm used to train classifiers, but instead a family of algorithms that are used. This group of algorithms is based on a common principle: that all naïve Bayes classifiers are independent of the value of any other feature in the model. An easy way to understand this would be to look at this example: let's say fruit is considered a grape if it is green, round, and about 1" in diameter.

A naïve Bayes classifier would consider each of these features to independently contribute to the probability of this fruit is a grape, regardless of any correlations that might exist between the three features described. So, even if there were a plausible correlation that confirmed the findings, it would not be considered in the naïve Bayes classifier algorithms.

The naïve Bayes classifier is trained as a supervised learning algorithm, because it requires a human to input parameters that allow it to identify the probability of something. Without a human being able to input these independent values, the classifier has no way of receiving knowledge and therefore no way of functioning. This particular algorithm cannot be trained to identify knowledge based on examples, so it has no way of becoming an unsupervised algorithm at this point in time. Furthermore, it has no purpose of becoming an unsupervised algorithm, since other algorithms would likely be more effective in an unsupervised setting, such as artificial neural networks.

In this chapter, we are going to dig deeper into what the naïve Bayes classifier really is, how it works, and when and why someone would use it. Despite how niche it is, this particular algorithm does have very useful applications making it incredibly effective in the right setting.

What Is the *Naïve Bayes Classifier* Algorithm?

Classifiers in general are machine learning models that are used to discriminate different objects based on certain features in the object. This way, they can classify, or separate, those objects based on a specific set of similarities and group them together for greater purposes, such as formulating statistics or probabilities.

The naïve Bayes classifier is no different, being that it is also a probabilistic machine learning model that is used to classify different objects. The naïve Bayes classifier differs only in the fact that it uses the Bayes Theorem to work, over any other model that may be presented.

How Does This Algorithm Work?

Not unlike other classifiers, the naïve Bayes classifier is a probabilistic machine learning model that can be used to classify things. This essentially means that, once it is programmed, it will organize things into specific categories and groups for the user depending on what they needed things to be categorized for. In order for this classifier to work, it requires the Bayes Theorem calculation.

This particular calculation is as follows:

$$P(A|B) = \frac{P(B|A)P(A)}{P(B)}$$

In this particular theorem, you can discover the probability of **A** happening based on the fact that **B** occurred. In other words, **A** cannot happen if **B** does not happen first. In the Bayes Theorem case, **A** represents the hypothesis and **B** represents the evidence.

The theorem will first read the evidence (**B**) in order to produce a hypothesis (**A**). In this particular theorem, it is assumed that the predictors and features are independent, which means that the presence of one does not affect the other. For example, in a spam filter in an email program, features such as: swear words, certain phishing words, and certain email handles could all be considered spam. However, all three would not need to be present for the email to be classified as spam. So long as one of the three was identified in the email being sent, it would be considered spam even if the other two were not represented in it.

Technically, there are different types of naïve Bayes classifiers. This is because naïve Bayes classifiers are more of a family of algorithms, rather than a single algorithm. Each type of naïve Bayes classifier will perform a different function and be used in a different setting and, depending on what is being done, a person may need to use two or more naïve Bayes classifier algorithms in order to complete their required task. The different types of the naïve Bayes classifiers include: the multinomial naïve Bayes, the Bernoulli naïve Bayes, and the Gaussian naïve Bayes.

Multinomial Naïve Bayes

The multinomial naïve Bayes is primarily used for document classification problems. For example, it can identify whether a document belongs to a specific category based on the factors relevant to that unique document. If it were, let's say, a news article, the multinomial naïve Bayes could accurately determine whether that article was best represented by sports, technology, politics, or otherwise. In this particular naïve Bayes classifier, the decision is made based on the frequency of certain types of language being used in a document.

Bernoulli Naïve Bayes

The Bernoulli naïve Bayes classifier is similar to the multinomial naïve Bayes classifier, except that the predictors are Boolean variables. This means that the parameters used to predict the class variable may only be a "yes" or a "no." For example, the parameter might be, does the word *"soccer"* exist in the text? If the answer is yes, it would be classified under one category. If it was no, it would be classified under a different category.

Gaussian Naïve Bayes

The gaussian naïve Bayes classifier is an algorithm that is used to identify a continuous value that is not discrete. In this case, the values are present but there is no clear classifier that determines how much those particular values are present, so the gaussian naïve Bayes classifier uses a certain set of parameters to essentially measure those values and classify the represented asset accordingly.

When Should This Algorithm be Used?

The naïve Bayes classifiers are a very niche type of classifier that is best used in specific settings, too. The two most common applications of the naïve Bayes algorithm in today's world include sorting documents in large filing systems, and sorting out spam and priority filters in various internet mailing applications, such as emails or social media messenger applications.

Filing Documents

When it comes to filing documents, the naïve Bayes classifier can be used to essentially determine which categories a document fits best under so that they can be organized accordingly. For businesses that use a lot of online documentation applications and that store multiple files in the online space, such as on cloud storage, the naïve Bayes algorithm can automatically store their files based on certain classifiers. The goal of the naïve Bayes algorithm would be for the classifiers to effectively store documents in a logical, meaningful, and useful manner that supports them in being found at a later date. If they are filed properly, they will be organized and easy to identify. A great example of large online filing networks would be news outlets. Some news outlets may manually sort their articles on their website, whereas others may employ the use of a naïve Bayes algorithm to ensure that their articles are being sorted and organized properly.

In these cases, they will likely create a clause that states that the file can be saved in a pre-selected number of archives and folders so that it can be found more effectively. This way, it is properly stored and it is more likely to be found by interested readers.

Spam and Priority Filters

Another common way the naïve Bayes classifier is used is when it comes to spam and priority filters. Spam filters are the most common and longest standing filters out there when it comes to the computer, as they have been used to sort and file spam email messages and other spam content in separate folders away from primary folders. This way, users are less likely to see spam content and will not have to filter through all of that content. In other words, it ensures that they are likely to see what matters and that they are unlikely to see anything else that may be sent to them by spam folks.

More recently, companies like Google have included additional filters in their platforms like Gmail. These additional filters help to prioritize or organize content that is being emailed to people so that people are easily able to sort through their mail without manually having to do it themselves. These different filters are generally: personal, promotional, and social. By organizing content accordingly, users are able to easily sort through their emails without having to manually change the labels of different emails in order to do so. For many, this has made navigating email much easier and less overwhelming, since many tend to have a large amount of promotional or social media related emails being sent to their inboxes on a regular basis.

This way, their personal or more important messages are not being buried under these less important and often less looked at messages.

Chapter 9: Random Forests

Random forests are another form of a classification system, similar to the naïve Bayes classification system, but structured more like the decision tree model. When you are using this classification system, information will continue to be classified but will help you come up with answers to the decisions that you may have to make. When it comes to big data sets, this can be helpful in identifying plausible solutions for overcoming challenges or reaching certain goals with the use of those data sets. When you look at the random forest algorithm, it looks as though you see multiple smaller decision trees lumped together into one larger tree. They are almost exactly the same in appearance, however the way they are established, the information they contain, and the purpose of these forests is somewhat different from a standard decision tree algorithm.

What Are *Random Forests?*

Random forests are a type of tree learning method that can be used by machine learning technology to complete certain decision-making tasks. A random forest is a form of standard data mining protocol that is able to scale and transform features of values. With that being said, random forests are more finicky than decision trees as they can include irrelevant and random values that may make the outcome less favorable than what the individual was looking for.

If the tree is developed properly, however, the tree will be more effective at producing accurate and meaningful results that can then be used for a number of different features.

The thing to be most cautious about when it comes to random forests is trees that are grown very deep, or ones where every possible sub-decision is recognized and included in the model. In many cases, a lot of these decisions become irrelevant and are not useful in detecting what the likely outcome would be because they lead too far away from the initial decision and the initial goal.

By identifying this information and pruning it, however, one can use a random forest to create decision trees that are effective in helping them reach their goals and make the stronger decision based on the data sets they are working with.

The fundamental concept behind the random forest network is that crowds present a large amount of wisdom. In other words, the more knowledge you have, the more knowledge you have. By creating several decision trees and grouping them together in a random forest, data can be presented in massive amounts of different ways, leading researchers or data scientists through different possible outcomes and showing them things that are worth noting. Typically, the decision trees in the random forest are uncorrelated, which is why the algorithm got the term "random forest" in the first place. These uncorrelated trees provide information that outperforms any individual decision tree by giving researchers plenty to think about, factor in, and use toward making their final decisions.

As a result, they are able to get as close to accurate as possible when it comes to deciding the proper way to proceed with a given problem that they are trying to solve, or goal they are trying to achieve.

How Do *Random Forests* Work?

The low or limited correlation between decision trees in the random forest is key to making this particular algorithm work. A great metaphor to relate this to in order to help you understand how random forests work and protect the results of their findings is through considering an investment portfolio. In the finance industry, traders will invest in multiple different stocks as a way to refrain from putting all of their eggs in one basket, so to speak. This way, if one of their investments does not work as planned and they lose money on it, they still have several other investments earning them money and their money is essentially protected. In this case, the protection is achieved by distributing the funds around to make sure that they are not all at risk of one single threat. When it comes to random forest trees, the same concept is applied.

By using multiple different decision trees, the random forest is able to draw multiple conclusions and use them in a way to ensure that the decisions being made are protected by the other decisions around it. In other words, one flawed decision tree is unlikely to destroy an entire decision if there are three others that have offset the flaw.

The more decision trees you make that can help you come up with your decision, the more success you are going to have in offsetting the risk of something being wrong so that your findings are more accurate. The trees essentially protect each other from their individual errors, so long as they are not constantly moving in the same direction, or overlapping in input too much.

In order to create a random forest, a person needs: some actual signal in their features so that the models they build are using those features. This way, they do better at random guessing. And, predictions and errors made by the individual trees that have low correlations to each other. So, if a random forest is generated and the majority of the trees say the same general thing in terms of their predictions and errors, chances are the trees are too similar to effectively execute the purpose of the random forest. However, if you can see how the results all work together to produce a greater concept, then you have likely executed the random forest perfectly and you will find yourself getting everything that you need out of this particular algorithm.

During the training process, random forests need to learn from a random sample of data points. This means that these samples are not correlating too significantly in any way. They are generally drawn with replacement, which is known as bootstrapping. This essentially means that the samples are going to be used multiple times in a single tree sometimes due to the nature of what they are and how they fit into the decision making process. In this case, although one single tree will have a high variance from other trees in the forest, all of the trees will have a low variance when you consider the forest as a whole. This randomization ensures that the trees are different enough to support the algorithm, but not so different that they are no longer relevant to the decision that the individual is attempting to make. When the time to test comes, the random forest predictions are made by averaging the predictions of each of the decision trees in the random forest.

The average of the predictions is then known as *bagging*, which essentially means that they are putting all of the information together in a way that creates one final outcome. Another more technical term for bagging is *bootstrap aggregate*.

When it comes to random forests, you can assume that a massive amount of data can rapidly be accumulated if things are not put within certain parameters. After all, using an entire forest of decision trees can lead to nearly endless possibilities and therefore more data than anyone wants, or needs, to use.

Rather than having excessive trees that ultimately take away from the quality of the forest, scientists ensure that each tree is only able to create so many subsets. This way, it can consider a limited number of features and come up with a limited number of decisions, based on what the scientist or programmer has outlined. This prevents the trees from becoming overpopulated, and maintains the high diversity between trees to avoid massive overlap which can lead to muddied results.

Typically, each tree will be limited to four subsets, although that may be increased or decreased depending on the unique set of circumstances and what the programmer needs from that tree.

Aside from these additional rules and features of the random forest concept, random forests are still very much like decision trees. After all, this particular algorithm is made up of several decision trees. This means that, aside from bagging, the trees are all read in the same manner and the outcome is still the same. The only difference is that the reading of a random forest is done when you take the averages of all of the results, rather than having one simple and straightforward result delivered to you through one single decision tree.

When Should *Random Forests* be Used?

Based on the nature of random forests, they are used in virtually any situation where a decision tree might be used. They are especially helpful when there is an enormous amount of data in question that needs to be represented by the tree and, while the data does correlate in some ways, it may not correlate in all ways. By having a random forest, you can represent all of your data and still come up with plausible solutions for any problems you may be facing when it comes to data or data sciences.

Because of how interchangeable the two tend to be, you might think there is ultimately no reason for a decision tree and that people should exclusively use random forests instead. Naturally, it would make sense to lean toward using the algorithm that provides the most accuracy and the best results, and can reflect greater amounts of data, right? Technically, yes. However, there are some cases where using a random forest would be far too excessive for a situation, just like there are some cases where using a single decision tree would just not make sense.

A great way to see this would be to use a boat as a reference. You would not want to navigate a river in a yacht any more than you would want to navigate the ocean in a kayak, right? The same goes for decision trees and random forests.

When you have a limited amount of data and the results of the algorithm are important but not critical, a decision tree is ideal. These trees do not require massive amounts of data, nor do they take as much time to program and run as a random forest would.

As a result, they tend to serve as a much more effective solution for less intense, or less sensitive areas of programming where a decision is made but there are no terrible risks or threats that will arise if absolute accuracy is not achieved.

A great example of the application of a decision tree specifically would be in business, when businesses are looking for a solution in a certain marketing strategy or a new way to reach their customers.

In these unique circumstances, the information is important but there is nothing sensitive about it, and being slightly off in the results would not be detrimental to the success of the company. Instead, it would simply provide more data for them to run again in the future when they were ready to create a new strategy for further implementation and growth.

Random forests, on the other hand, are far more high tech and are ideal to use in sensitive situations or situations where there needs to be a high level of accuracy in a large amount of data. If, for example, you were running data about a government organization or an entire population, a random forest would be more accurate as it holds enough space to run that massive amount of data. As well, the accuracy of it would be more effective for these scenarios as the data tends to be more sensitive and the results need to be more accurate to avoid possible challenges in the outcomes.

Aside from areas with sensitive information, or with sensitive nature, random forests should also be used if there are massive amounts of data.

For example, a massive corporation like Wal-Mart or Target would be unlikely to benefit from a simple decision tree because there is far too much information within their businesses to effectively run it through a decision tree for adequate results. Likewise, a bank, a charitable organization, a government organization, or any other company or organization with high levels of data would not benefit from having all of that information stored in a single small decision tree. Not only are these trees less accurate, but they also do not have the capacity to store as much information as an entire random forest would. For that reason, a random forest is ideal in the case of large amounts of data needing to be processed, too.

So, to summarize, you should use a decision tree if you do not require extremely accurate results *and* you do not have massive amounts of data to run.

Alternatively, you should use a random forest when you need extremely accurate results *or* you have massive amounts of data to process and you need an algorithm large enough to allow you to effectively process it all.

Chapter 10: Apriori Algorithm

The Apriori algorithm is a unique algorithm that was introduced in 1994 by R. Agrawal and R. Srikant. These two scientists developed an algorithm that is capable of identifying prior knowledge and using it to identify itemset properties in datasets using the Boolean association rule. This particular algorithm is used in data mining as a way to find out certain correlations and connections in items using previous information.

There are many practical ways that the Apriori algorithm has been used in the modern world, especially in business where this particular algorithm has supported corporations in skyrocketing their sales by identifying like items and pairing them together for discounts. The way that this algorithm has been used is often a joke amongst computer scientists and is known as the "diaper beer parable" which you will learn more about later in this very chapter.

In order to help you better understand the algorithm that is associated with the "diaper beer parable" we are going to look into what the Apriori algorithm is, how it works, and when or why it would be used. This way, you have a better understanding of this particular algorithm that has been incredibly effective in helping draw patterns and trends in item sets and datasets for large organizations.

What Is the *Apriori* Algorithm?

The Apriori algorithm has a very specific function, and that is to identify relevant association rules and frequent item sets in data. In other words, it is used to identify how two different items might correlate with each other, what connections can be drawn between these items, and what these connections mean. This is where the diaper beer parable comes from.

Back in the day, someone working at Wal-Mart decided to look back through sales data to identify what types of items people commonly bought together. This way, they could leverage these items to increase sales by advertising sales of one item around the other item, when the two items were frequently bought together. A great example of this would be with jam and bread. Frequently, those who bought jam were also buying bread at the same time, so they would advertise bread near the jam, and jam near the bread. This would happen both physically in the store, and in flyers that were being promoted to their customers. In a sense, this was a way for Wal-Mart to upsell their customers so that they could maximize their earnings.

While looking through the sales records, what the gentleman found was intriguing. Customers would typically buy diapers and beer at the same time. Although these two products have seemingly zero correlation, the data was undeniable: the two were paired together an incredible amount and therefore he was able to leverage one to encourage the purchase of the other. Thus, the diaper beer parable was discovered.

This particular example showcases exactly how the Apriori algorithm works, too. The algorithm looks through data and identifies seemingly random pairs that have distinct and undeniable correlations. This data mining allows new understandings of data to be reached so that new developments can be discovered. In the case of Wal-Mart and other corporations, this has led to massive increases in sales due to a better understanding of what customers are typically buying together and how products can be better marketed to encourage their purchase together. In other areas, this important correlation can also help data scientists, researchers, and other relevant individuals identify the relations between two seemingly random items in a data set so that this knowledge can be used to improve various other applications.

How Does This Algorithm Work?

The Apriori algorithm works using association rules. Association rule learning is a well-explored method of machine learning that is designed to help determine relations amongst variables in massive sets of data.

Ideally, users should be able to upload massive amounts of data and the algorithm will run through it all and make these correlations and provide them at the end as an "answer" to the data that has been run. This way, the individual or organization can see these distinct correlations.

When the Apriori algorithm has been programmed, it works as follows. First, the user uploads a dataset into the algorithm in a way that isolates that dataset as a single group. For example, in a retail company a single receipt with a unique ID would represent one dataset. Every item that is a part of that dataset is then considered an item. So, for example, bread, butter, and eggs would all count as different items.

These would all be grouped together in the algorithm through the dataset, but the algorithm would begin to recognize the same items amongst all of the datasets. So, if the next receipt included eggs, potatoes, and milk, the algorithm would recognize these as two different datasets *and* recognize that both datasets included eggs. While this example only contains two receipts, the true Apriori algorithm would feature hundreds, thousands, hundreds of thousands, or even millions of individual datasets that each featured their own unique items. These could represent retail items, demographics, monetary values, or any other number of data depending on what the individual using the algorithm is attempting to discover. Ideally, in order to get a strong and accurate representation of their findings, the individual using the Apriori algorithm should have, or have access to, large amounts of data to ensure that their findings are accurate.

Using too small of an amount of data could lead to the findings not being accurate because it may be more up to chance than anything else.

Once the massive amount of data has been inputted, the algorithm is designed to require a certain level of parables to occur before it recognizes it as a plausible pair. For example, 1/10 instances of a parable would not be recognized at all by the Apriori algorithm, but 4/10 or higher instances of a parable might be recognized, depending on how that unique software was programmed by the developer.

The benefit of the Apriori algorithm is that it can pair together multiple different items and recognize the connection between groups of items, too.

For example, it may recognize that people who buy bras and underwear are also likely to buy socks, or people who are religious and in the middle class are more likely to attend church on a consistent basis. This way, it can make extremely accurate findings based on the information being uploaded into the system. After it has found these groups of relevant items, the Apriori algorithm moves into what is called confidence.

This means that the algorithm must have confidence in a rule to confirm that said rule is likely going to be accurate and that the findings of the algorithm are accurate, too. In order to reflect confidence, the algorithm will showcase the exact statistics relating to the associations or parables it has made. Often, this is shown as a percentage so that the user can see an exact percentage of how frequently those items were paired together, allowing them to get a better understanding of how relevant these parables are.

If the percentage is low, chances are the parable is random and does not mean much in the way of how people are actually shopping. If, however, the percentage is fairly high, chances are the parable is not all that random and if it is exploited they can actually increase the percentage. Typically, this exploitation is only done to improve desirable results, and is never used in an unethical manner to avoid causing unethical interference into people's lives. For example, a retailer might pair two items together to improve sales numbers, but a government is unlikely to use their findings of people who are religious and middle class to increase the number of churchgoers in their riding.

When Should This Algorithm be Used?

The Apriori algorithm is actually used in many ways in our current world as it has the capacity to shine a light into certain pairings that would otherwise be unknown to the people looking into this data. Using this algorithm, organizations are able to create more relevant and enjoyable experiences for the people they represent or support. The algorithm can give them a better understanding of who they are supporting, and what those individuals need, want, or care about.

Currently, the Apriori algorithm is frequently used in marketing and commerce, however it is also used in statistical analysis companies where they are trying to gain a better understanding of the statistics they are researching. National statistical organizations, for example, who keep track of certain public statistics will regularly use the Apriori algorithm to ensure that they have accurately drawn conclusions in all their findings. It is also used in companies that are responsible for taking care of electric motors, which tends to be surprising to many people.

Marketing

In marketing, the Apriori algorithm is used to support people in the same way that it helped the man at Wal-Mart increase sales in diapers and beer. By allowing marketers to identify correlations between two item sets, they are able to identify new methods for marketing to the people that they are selling to.

On social media, the Apriori algorithm is used to show users advertisements that are relevant to their interests. For example, if the Apriori algorithm finds that people who regularly search dogs and horses tend to also buy buffalo plaid shirts, it could advertise buffalo plaid shirts that individual. The more these correlations are found, the more relevant targeted advertising becomes and, therefore, the more likely people are to act on that advertising and actually pay the company. For social media networks, this means companies are more likely to keep advertising through them, which ensures that their revenue stays up or even increases over time.

In email marketing, the Apriori algorithm can help companies identify what their subscribers tend to read about the most so that they can start to write targeted emails that are more likely to get opened and clicked on. This way, they are more likely to have an impact on their email marketing efforts and, therefore, they are more likely to earn money this way.

When it comes to offline marketing, the Apriori algorithm is used in exactly the same way that the Wal-Mart guy used it. Marketers look through sales statistics and use them to identify ways that they can improve their sales strategies by finding offline marketing methods that reflect their findings. For example, grouping similar items together in flyers, or on instore posters where certain products are being promoted.

Commerce

In commerce, the Apriori algorithm is frequently used as a way to identify opportunities for growth, or new products or services that could be added or developed to help improve revenue in a business.

For example, if it was discovered that two items were frequently bought together with a specific product, and that this occurrence was high, that company could develop more products in that particular area and focus on improving that particular service. This way, the people who are already purchasing these products and services together are more likely to purchase even more based on the developments within the business.

Statistical Analysis Companies

Statistical analysis companies are necessary for helping us keep track of historical statistical data so that we can understand the state and evolution of our own society. These companies frequently store data reflecting demographics, health analysis, ecosystems, and more. By preserving this data, they are then able to ensure that it is available when the data is needed at future dates.

For example, when new research studies are being completed, researchers can look back at this historical data to create the foundation of their research, and to validate why they have come to this conclusion. They can also use this data to start creating theories that they can begin to follow. Often, this data will serve in many ways throughout the research process to help the researchers understand more about the specific area they are researching. Because of how these statistical companies work, the Apriori algorithm is highly useful to them. Using the algorithm, they can take their existing raw statistics and data and run it through the system to find out even more information, effectively creating even more statistics or data for people to use. For example, they might run information that shows that the middle class millennials are less likely to purchase a home by 30 years old than the middle class baby boomers, or other similar findings.

Through the development of their statistics, these companies are able to create a better understanding of the landscape of our society now, and in the historical past. As a result, future researchers are able to fall back on this knowledge to create clear paths from how we have evolved or advanced through the years.

Mechanics

In mechanics, the Apriori algorithm is frequently used as a way to ensure that mechanics have effectively looked over every aspect of an engine and ensured its safety. It can also be used to troubleshoot engines when something is going wrong and the mechanic cannot find the answer. Using the Apriori algorithm, if the mechanic can identify one clear issue, they can look at the data to identify what that issue tends to be associated with. This way, if it is something that they could not draw a conclusion to using common sense, the conclusion is drawn using the Apriori algorithm. Then, rather than cars being deemed irreparable or problems deemed unresolvable, the mechanic can go ahead and identify what needs to be addressed.

In addition to helping mechanics fix engines, it can also help them identify common problems in certain engine types. Through that, they can stay informed as to what to look out for, and also inform people who own the vehicle attached to that engine as to what they should look out for, too. In situations where the instances are high and the findings are dangerous, they can also issue safety recalls ensuring that no one is left driving an unfit or unsafe vehicle.

Service Engineers

In addition to engines, the Apriori algorithm can be applied in the exact same manner for other service engineers, and even IT agents or individuals who are responsible for building and fixing things.

134

Using the Apriori algorithm, engineers can educate themselves on problems to look out for, as well as things to consider when it comes to building or repairing different pieces of technology. If they find that the correlations are often catastrophic or dangerous, they can also begin to identify new ways to overcome those problems to ensure that they are no longer causing issues for the individuals who own the technology. Or, they can prevent the technology from being mass produced until it has been fixed and is fit to go out.

136

Chapter 11: Linear and Logistic Regression

Linear and logistic regression are similar, but they are not entirely the same. In this chapter, we are going to explore what linear and logistic regression are, how they work, and why they are used. It is important to understand that both linear and logistic regression can be used in similar settings, however in some linear regression will make more sense, whereas in others, logistic regression will make more sense. The key difference is how many possible values exist in the regression that is being completed. Linear regression has an infinite number of possible values, whereas logistic regression has a limited number of possible values. As a result, both are somewhat different and are shown slightly differently on graphs, too. Linear regression tends to be shown as a single solid line that is straight and gradually increases, whereas logistic regression tends to be shown as a curved line that increases based on the values being represented by the graph.

Using one graph in place of the other would be a mistake as it would essentially "break" the output number. In both linear and logic regression, the output should never be negative or greater than one. If these two scenarios were to occur, the result would be wrong which would mean that you were not receiving accurate or sound information from your regression.

For this reason, it is important that you use the right regression algorithm for the right purpose, to avoid having your values turned up wrong or inconclusive.

Exploring how each algorithm works, when to use it, and what it's purpose is in the first place is an important element of understanding the value of this particular algorithm. Once again, this particular algorithm is one of the most basic machine learning algorithms, and it is used across many different areas in machine learning. For that reason, it is important that you take the time to educate yourself on how it works and put it to work accordingly.

What is *Linear Regression*?

Linear regression is a form of predictive analysis that measures probabilities to identify the likelihood of something happening. The idea of regression is for this particular algorithm to examine two things: the quality of certain predictor variables, and the significance of certain predictor variables. First and foremost, the predictor variables need to be able to effectively predict the outcome variable, otherwise they are not going to be effective in helping you with your predictions and probabilities.

Second, you need to know that the variables you are using are significant predictors of the outcome variable, as well as how they impact the outcome variable. If you do not know these two pieces of information, you will not have an effective linear regression algorithm. With these two pieces of information in tow, the linear regression algorithm is able to explain the relationship between one dependent variable and one or more independent variables, ultimately leading to the development of a probability measure.

This way, you can start to see the likelihood of something happening, and how the dependent variables support or lead to the independent variables taking place.

Linear regression algorithms can be amongst some of the more challenging algorithms to learn about because they do tend to include so many variables, and the variables need to be qualified in order to make sure that they are good enough to use with the particular calculations you are running through the algorithm. If these variables are low quality or ineffective, they are not going to be able to help you create the outcome you desire, or the results of your linear regression algorithm may be inconclusive or inaccurate.

Based on the number of variables that can be included in linear regression, it is understandable that there are also multiple different ways that this algorithm can be used to understand the variables and create your calculations. In fact, there are six different types of linear regression algorithms that can be used to help seek your probability answers, depending on what types of information you have available to run through the algorithm.

These six linear regression types include: simple linear regression, multiple linear regression, logistic regression, ordinal regression, multinomial regression, and discriminant analysis. While we will talk more in depth about logistic regression later in this chapter, due to it being a significant form of linear regression, let's take a moment to explore each of the other types of linear regression, too. Aside from simple linear regression, the other four types of linear regression tend to be more complex, but are still useful algorithms to know about.

Multiple Linear Regression

Multiple linear regression essentially means that multiple independent variables are being assessed in the algorithm. As with all forms of linear regression, multiple linear regression only takes into account one dependent variable.

Multiple linear regression is the easiest next step up from simple linear regression, which is a form of linear regression that only measures one dependent variable, and one independent variable.

For both simple linear regression and multiple linear regression, the independent variable must be either an interval, ratio, or dichotomous and the dependent variable needs to be either an interval or ratio.

Ordinal Regression

Ordinal regression is a form of linear regression that involves just one dependent variable, and one or more independent variables. With that being said, the dependent variable should be ordinal, and the independent variable(s) should be nominal or dichotomous in nature. Ordinal regression can feature any number of independent variables, depending on what data is being run through the algorithm.

Multinominal Regression

Multinominal regression is another form of regression that features one or more independent variables, and one dependent variable. In the case of multinominal regression, the dependent variable must always be nominal. The independent variables can be either interval, ratio, or dichotomous.

Discriminant Analysis

Lastly, discriminant analysis is a form of linear regression that features one dependent variable, and one or more independent variables. For discriminant analysis, the dependent variable should be nominal, and the independent variable should be either an interval or ratio. When a researcher is choosing which type of linear regression they are going to use, they start by determining model fitting. This essentially means that they take a look at what data they have and what their goals are, and they determine which method is going to best serve them in achieving those goals.

By fitting the method to their data, they are able to get the best results that lead to them experiencing more accuracy and success in their research using linear regression.

How Does *Linear Regression* Work?

For the purpose of this explanation, we are going to discuss simple linear regression, which features one dependent variable and just one independent variable. With that being said, all additional forms of linear regression work in this exact same manner, and they can be used to perform the necessary functions based on what you are looking for in your data, and what type of data you have.

The purpose of linear regression is to model the relationship between one or more variables, so that is exactly what you are going to do with linear regression. Each linear regression model is trained with formulas that indicate what the model is supposed to do. This way, the model knows what variables it is looking at and what relationships it is looking for. The goal of training the model and using it is to see the relationship between independent variables and dependent variables. For example, features versus labels.

Once a linear regression model is trained, a user can begin inputting data into the system that will ultimately be run through the algorithm and represented in a series of relationships and values. These relationships and values will determine probabilities and predictive scenarios based on the relationship something shares with something else. This is a great way to reinforce assumptions or identify areas where the independent variables are more likely to support the dependent variable, so that the user can identify the best possible way to move forward.

Unlike decision trees or other tree based learning algorithms, linear regression will not give you a series of different outcomes or draw you down a path of identifying what you could possibly do. Instead, a linear regression algorithm will identify the probability of something happening based on you pre-emptively identifying what that something is and then inputting it into the algorithm. This way, you can reinforce whether or not that will actually be true or whether it will work or not, and you can move forward from there.

In other words, if you do not already have a theory and some data surrounding that theory, you are unlikely to see any benefit in using a linear regression model.

When Should *Linear Regression* be Used?

A linear regression model should be used when you already have a basic understanding as to what needs to be done and what can be done to reach a certain goal. Once you have this basic understanding, you can input this information into a linear regression model using a dependent variable and then one or more independent variables in the form of nominals, ratios, intervals, or dichotomy. Then, the algorithm will run through the information you have to create conclusive results that determine whether or not a certain outcome is likely to be achieved. If you do not already have a basic idea of what goes together, however, you will likely want to run your data through other algorithms first to begin to create a theory or a hypothesis.

From there, you can then take your findings and run it through a linear regression algorithm to identify the best possible route, and how good that route actually is. In other words, this is a great way to discover which theory is correct and to which degree that theory is correct.

In real life, linear regression can be used on things like budgeting, agriculture, ordering retail suppliers, and many other things. Essentially, anything you can use linear regression charts on anything that features two unique variables on a graph.

Budgeting

In budgeting, you can use linear regression to help you identify how much money you should expect to spend on something based on what you have experienced in the past, and what you need to do in the future. For example, let's say you are driving a car and that car requires gas in order to be able to go anywhere. If you were using linear regression, you could track how much money you put into your tank each time you fill up, and how far you drive before filling up again. In this case, you would start to be able to identify how many miles you get per gallon, and how frequently you need to put gas in your car. With this knowledge, your gas (dependent variable) is being measured against your miles driven (independent variable).

You, then, must identify how much the dependent variable relates to the independent variable, or how much gas you need to purchase in order to make it a certain distance. With the answer to this equation in mind, you could then identify how many miles you needed to drive, and multiply that by the dollar value you came up with your linear regression chart. Through that, you would know how much money you need to budget for gas in order to reach a certain distance in your travels.

Agriculture

In agriculture, linear regression can help farmers identify what types of variables are going to affect things such as their crops. For example, let's say a farmer was looking into their crop yield and wanted to know how much certain independent variables affected his crop yield.

In this case, he could run an analysis where he identifies how much these independent variables have affected crop yield in the past to get an understanding of what is likely to affect his crop yield.

He might test against amount of rainfall, amount of sunshine, pesticides used, farming practices used, and other independent variables to see how much these independent variables have affected his crop yield. As a result, he would be able to get an accurate understanding as to what would affect his yield, and possibly be able to create a plan to offset anything that may negatively impact his yield.

Retail – Ordering

In retail, linear regression can be used to help companies identify how much products they should be ordering with each order. They would be able to measure the number of products sold against how long it took for those products to sell. In this case, the dependent variable would be the passing of a set period of time (the time between orders) and the independent variable would be the number of products sold in that timeframe. Through this algorithm, the retailer could identify how many products were consistently being sold in that time period so that they could identify how many products they needed to order.

This way, they order enough to keep up with supply and demand, but not so much that they find themselves buried in excess products that their customers are not purchasing.

What is *Logistical Regression?*

Logistical regression is a form of linear regression, but it is different in that there are a fixed number of probabilities that can be measured by the logistic regression algorithm. This limited number of probabilities is based on the variables being inputted and the number of existing probabilities relating to these variables. Logistic regression should always be used when the dependent variable is measured in the algorithm is dichotomous, or binary. This means that it is represented in a series of 1's and 0's. Logistic regression specifically is used to explain the relationship between one binary dependent variable and one or more nominal, ordinal, interval, or ratio-level independent variables. Based on the nature of this particular form of linear regression, this algorithm can be more challenging to read than other linear regression algorithms. As a result, some people may prefer to use a tool like the Intellectus Statistics tool to help them interpret the output in plain English. Without it, one must have a solid understanding of coding and binary language to understand exactly what the algorithm is trying to tell them.

Logistic regression is used to estimate the parameters of a logistic model, much in the same way that other forms of linear regression are used. The purpose is to identify the probability of a specific outcome. Again, like other forms of linear regression, it will not perform statistical classification, nor will it point toward multiple different outcomes.

The sole purpose of logistic regression is to validate the strength of a relationship between a dependent and independent variable to see how likely it is that one will affect the other. Typically, the individual running this system already knows that one will affect the other, which is why they are running the two variables together through the algorithm in the first place.

How Does *Logistic Regression* Work?

Logistic regression works by taking into account the dependent and independent variables that are at play in any given scenario. The entire practice is performed exactly as simple linear regression is performed, however the goals will ultimately be different. As well, the types of variables being used are different, particularly with the fact that the dependent variable is going to be dichotomous, or binary.

Once the dichotomous dependent variable has been observed, the individual running the logistic regression model needs to identify what their independent variables are. From there, they can turn those independent variables into ratios, nominals, ordinals, or intervals so that they can be run through the algorithm properly.

Assuming that everything has been inputted properly, the entire process of logistic regression will be exactly the same. You will be placing your probability on a graph with your dependent variable on the left side and your independent variable on the bottom of your graph, and mapping out your data points on a chart.

Or, more specifically, the machine learning model will be doing this for you based on the information you have inputted into the system. From there, it will plot out the average path of probability, showing you what is likely to be true. Unlike plain linear regression models, the logistic regression model can be shown with a curved line. With that being said, the line should always be curving up and to the right, starting at the bottom left side of the graph. If it is curving in any other direction, the algorithm has not been effective and it needs to be retrained or the information inputted needs to be reviewed to ensure that it is being run properly.

When Should *Logistic Regression* be Used?

Logistic regression is mostly used in machine learning technology that is related to medical and social fields. A great example of it being actively used is represented in the Trauma and Injury Severity Score (TRISS) which is typically used to predict the likelihood of mortality in a patient who has been significantly injured. Using logistic regression, they can predict the likelihood of whether or not someone is going to die based on the trauma or injuries they have sustained, across other independent variables that may be highlighted in their unique case. Another way that the medical field uses logistic regression is to identify the likelihood of someone developing something like diabetes, coronary heart disease, or another illness based on the observed characteristics of the patient, such as their age, weight, sex, and results on varying tests they may have taken. In these applications, logistic regression is incredibly useful in helping doctors identify what measures need to be taken to help a patient, and to what degree those measures need to be taken. In other words, they are incredibly useful in helping doctors essentially choose a diagnostic path for a patient depending on what sort of health issues they are presently facing.

In socioeconomics, the logistic regression model can be used to identify the likelihood of people needing to join the labor force, being able to own a home, being able to manage a mortgage, or various other things that may be relevant to a person's lifestyle. Through taking a dependent, such as what they are looking into a person's likelihood of experiencing, and applying independent variables such as their demographic classification, the logistic regression algorithm can identify probabilities.

Conclusion

Congratulations on completing *Machine Learning for Beginners!* This book was written to be a helpful guide for anyone curious about learning more about machine learning and its many applications. From covering topics ranging from what machine learning is and how it is used, to discovering what types of algorithms and complex systems are run through machine learning devices, I hope you are starting to feel confident in your understanding of machine learning.

When most people think of machine learning, they either have no idea what it is, or they automatically think about artificial intelligence in the form of a robotic species that rivals humans. While these fascinating subspecies may one day exist as the result of machine learning developments, right now the primary focus is on how machine learning programs can become excellent at very specific tasks. Most machine learning technology is developed in such a way that it is excellent at performing one or, at most, two tasks.

By focusing entire technology on one single task, they can ensure that it runs that task perfectly, and that it does not get confused between the tasks that it is trying to accomplish. While simple computing software like the one that runs your computer can easily run multiple programs at once with little chance of crashing, the technology that is used to run machine learning technology is far more complex.

As researchers study it, they strive to keep the algorithms mostly separate, or specifically focused on completing just one goal, on minimizing room for error.

It is likely that as we become more familiar with machine learning technology and more educated in the algorithms, we will start to see more and more machines completing multiple tasks, rather than just one. At this point, that is the long term goal for many scientists who want to see these machines becoming more effecient, and requiring less hardware. After all, the hardware used to run some of these machines is not always the greenest technology, so the fewer hardware casings that technology needs to be stored in, the less of a footprint the technology sector will have on the planet.

I hope that in reading this book you have begun to feel confident in your understanding of machine learning. This topic is incredibly complex and diving into any one special area of it in a single book would be nearly impossible. Even computer scientists spend years studying multiple texts and research papers, trying to learn more about these machine learning programs and how they work. With that being said, *Machine Learning for Beginners* sought to put together the most important knowledge that any beginner should have to ensure that you had access to the best and most important knowledge for you.

As you move forward from this book, I hope that you will take the time to continue following the machine learning industry, or even consider dipping your own toes into it.

Machine learning is not like traditional computer science fields that are focused on human created and managed algorithms, but instead it is focused on learning how to develop machines that can perform various functions on their own.

With the proper training models and algorithms installed into these pieces of technology, these systems are already capable of performing incredible tasks.

It will be interesting to see where machine learning goes in the next few years, and decades, as computer scientists continue to explore this uncharted territory.

Already, anyone who has used any form of technology, or who has gone to a doctor or government office where technology was used has benefitted from the existence of machine learning protocol. This means that literally everyone in the modern world has, in one way or another, been impacted by it. This particular form of science sprung up in the mid-1900s and has rapidly grown in popularity and served to provide us with the basis of what might be the earliest stages of the machine learning revolution, or whatever future historians may call it. With the evolution and implementation of machine learning technology, life as we know it may change completely. We could likely see changes ranging from reduced need for people in the labor force, to better transportation technologies, and even better medical and screening technologies.

It is likely that, in time, no sector of our modern world will be without incredibly advanced, high powered machine learning technology that will change the way that the entire sector is run.

In the meantime, it will likely take time for this revolution to happen, as we are unlikely to see machine learning advance to the point where it would be ethical to overhaul most existing systems with it any time soon. Before that can happen, we will need to further develop the technology to make sure that it is reliable, accurate, and ethical in every single scenario. This way, when it begins to be used in areas with more sensitive data, such as government records, health records, bank records, or educational records, we can feel confident that it is going to function properly.

After all, we do not want sensitive records or documents leaking into the wrong hands and causing massive destruction to our society. Which, as dramatic as it might sound, is entirely possible and could be a complete catastrophe.

Before you go, I want to ask you one simple favor. If you enjoyed reading *Machine Learning for Beginners: A Complete and Phased Beginner's Guide to Learning and Understanding Machine Learning and Artificial Intelligence* and feel that it helped you understand machine learning more effectively, I ask that you please take the time to leave a review on Amazon Kindle. Your honest feedback and support would be greatly appreciated.

Thank you, and have fun exploring the world of machine learning! The possibilities truly are endless!

www.ingramcontent.com/pod-product-compliance
Lightning Source LLC
LaVergne TN
LVHW051241050326
832903LV00028B/2512